A Practical Guide to

Data Center Operations Management

AUERBACH Data Processing Management Library

James Hannan, Editor

•

Contributors To This Volume

Thomas J. Boyle
President, Marketing Technology Incorporated
Bronxville NY

Philip C. Cross
Vice President, Abraham & Straus, New York NY

Jagdish R. Dalal
Manager, Management Information Systems,
Brookhaven National Laboratory, Upton NY

Dale Dull
Assistant Manager, DP Division, County of Madison WI

Robert W. Edwards
Manager, Wood, Butkow, Kemp, and Partners Limited
Fairfax VA

Jerry Gitomer
Blue Bell PA

Dr. William A. Hansen
President, Training Development Corporation
Elk Grove Village IL

Edward J. Kirby
Systems Design Consultant, Sherborn MA

Herb Liebovitz
President, CRM Incorporated, Saddlebrook NJ

John W. Mentzer
Downingtown PA

Daniel A. Pagano
Vincentown NJ

Richard E. Petrelli
Vincentown NJ

Howard Schaeffer
Consultant, Newton NJ

Bryan Wilkinson
CISA, Teledyne Incorporated, Los Angeles CA

A Practical Guide to

Data Center Operations Management

Edited by James Hannan

AUERBACH Publishers Incorporated
Pennsauken NJ

VAN NOSTRAND REINHOLD COMPANY
New York Cincinnati Toronto London Melbourne

Copyright © 1982 by AUERBACH Publishers Inc

Library of Congress Catalog Card Number 82-11622

ISBN 0-442-20912-6

Printed in the United States of America

Published in the United States in 1982
by Van Nostrand Reinhold Company Inc
135 West 50th Street
New York NY 10020 USA

16 15 14 13 12 11 10 9 8 7 6 5 4 3 2 1

Library of Congress Cataloging in Publication Data
Main entry under title:

A Practical guide to data center operations management.

(Auerbach data processing management library ; 6)
1. Electronic data processing—Management. I. Hannan, James, 1946-   . II. Series.
QA76.9.M3P68   1982   001.64'068   82-11622
ISBN 0-442-20912-6 (pbk.)

Contents

Contents

Preface

In its relatively brief existence, the computer has emerged from the back rooms of most organizations to become an integral part of business life. Increasingly sophisticated data processing systems are being used today to solve increasingly complex business problems. As a result, the typical data processing function has become as intricate and specialized as the business enterprise it serves.

Such specialization places a strenuous burden on computer professionals. Not only must they possess specific technical expertise, they must understand how to apply their special knowledge in support of business objectives and goals. A computer professional's effectiveness and career hinge on how ably he or she manages this challenge.

To assist computer professionals in meeting this challenge, AUERBACH Publishers has developed the *AUERBACH Data Processing Management Library*. The series comprises eight volumes, each addressing the management of a specific DP function:

A Practical Guide to Data Processing Management
A Practical Guide to Programming Management
A Practical Guide to Data Communications Management
A Practical Guide to Data Base Management
A Practical Guide to Systems Development Management
A Practical Guide to Data Center Operations Management
A Practical Guide to EDP Auditing
A Practical Guide to Distributed Processing Management

Each volume contains well-tested, practical solutions to the most common and pressing set of problems facing the manager of that function. Supplying the solutions is a prominent group of DP practitioners—people who make their living in the areas they write about. The concise, focused chapters are designed to help the reader directly apply the solutions they contain to his or her environment.

AUERBACH has been serving the information needs of computer professionals for more than 25 years and knows how to help them increase their effectiveness and enhance their careers. The *AUERBACH Data Processing Management Library* is just one of the company's many offerings in this field.

James Hannan
Assistant Vice President
AUERBACH Publishers

Introduction

The data center has long served as the focal point of the DP function in most organizations. Mention data processing to the typical user, and he or she is likely to think first of the "computer room" and summon up images of blinking lights, whirling tapes, clattering printers, and bustling activity. Ask that same user whom he or she contacts when reports are late or terminal response times are slow, and the answer will probably be, "the operations department." It is particularly ironic, then, that despite the visibility of the data center and the level of activity it supports, the data center operations manager (DCOM) is virtually unknown outside the DP management group.

The DCOM's anonymity is largely attributable to the way in which operations has evolved. Once a back-room activity, it has since become a complex, production-oriented service function that must satisfy a growing and increasingly diverse number of user demands with systems designed and built by DP professionals outside the data center. Lacking direct control in both the user and systems areas, the DCOM often becomes more a reactive problem solver than a proactive manager. This volume of the *AUERBACH Data Processing Management Library* is designed to redress that imbalance.

We have commissioned an outstanding group of DP practitioners to share the benefits of their extensive and varied experience in operations. Our authors have written on a carefully chosen range of topics and have provided proven, practical advice for managing the data center operations function more productively.

In Chapter One, Philip C. Cross discusses the problem of organizing for data center productivity. He describes several techniques for effectively managing operations personnel and for organizing and tracking data center work flow.

A proven technique for increasing personnel productivity is a clearly defined career path. In most data centers, however, career path planning is seldom, if ever, done. Dr. William A. Hansen, in his "Career Planning in Operations," discusses the conditions that affect the performance and attitudes of operations people and suggests approaches to improving these conditions.

In addition to techniques for improving personnel productivity, several tools are available for increasing operational productivity; comprehensive, up-to-date documentation and an effective scheduling system are two of the most useful. In Chapter Three, Howard Schaeffer describes the types of documentation that are required and discusses criteria for their evaluation; he also provides detailed guidelines for developing a handbook for data center users. In Chapter Four, Daniel A. Pagano and Richard E. Petrelli discuss the planning process the DCOM should follow in choosing and implementing a scheduling system that will aid in allocating computer resources and improving work flow.

Another essential element in managing for greater productivity is effective control of data center operations, which stems from good planning. In his "Data Center Planning Checklist," Philip Cross presents a series of questions the DCOM should ask to determine the effectiveness of the data center planning function.

To facilitate management planning and control the DCOM must understand the concepts and process of budgeting. To that end, Jagdish R. Dalal provides an overview of the procedures used in developing and managing the data center budget in Chapter Six. In Chapter Seven, Edward J. Kirby surveys the politics of budget preparation and suggests ways in which the DCOM can deal with the strategic problems associated with budget approval.

A significant portion of any DCOM's budget is allocated to the purchase and maintenance of hardware. The primary criteria for selecting computer equipment are usually current and future user requirements and the performance characteristics of the hardware and software; however, the support provided by the vendor is an equally important consideration. The AUERBACH editorial staff provides a questionnarie in Chapter Eight to help the DCOM evaluate vendor support policies.

Evaluating equipment and support policies represents only part of the DCOM's interaction with vendors. After narrowing the choice of vendors, the DCOM must be prepared to strike the best possible deal. When negotiating a contract for equipment and services, no one has more at stake than the DCOM. To ensure that his interests are represented and to bring his DP expertise to bear, the DCOM should participate in the negotiating process. In his "Negotiating with Vendors," Dale Dull describes a team approach to negotiating that helps ensure that the contract is acceptable to both the DCOM and the company.

No matter how carefully selected, equipment and systems can fail; and even the most cost-effective service agreements can involve expensive service calls. Most such calls, however, result from poor maintenance practices and/or failure to check for correctable problems. In "What To Do Before You Call for Service," Jerry Gitomer alerts the DCOM to the potential sources of trouble, suggests ways of improving the working environment to minimize breakdowns, and outlines diagnostic procedures that can eliminate calling for service.

The data center often plays a crucial role in handling information concerning the organization's assets. Ensuring that this information is safe from both unintentional and deliberate misuse is one of the DCOM's major concerns. Separation of duties is a traditional control technique that can help the DCOM meet this goal. In Chapter Eleven, Bryan Wilkinson explains the concept of separation of duties, suggests how it should be applied in the data center, and discusses implementation costs and alternative control methods.

Data security software packages are another effective tool for protecting the organization's information assets. In order to select the proper package, the organization must establish security requirements, define the functional and technical criteria to be used in the evaluation, and conduct product evaluation and selection. In Chapter Twelve, Robert W. Edwards presents practical guidelines for specifying requirements and for evaluating and selecting data security software.

While improving personnel and operational productivity are the two most important factors in maintaining operations efficiency and effectiveness, the DCOM should not ignore environmental factors in the data center. A cluttered, sloppy center can reduce productivity and present serious security and safety problems. Similarly, such factors as air flow, air quality, and static can affect hardware operations and the health of data center personnel. In "Good Data Center Housekeeping," John W. Mentzer provides checklists for rating a data center's housekeeping effort and discusses ways to accomplish needed improvements. And in Chapter Fourteen, Herb Liebovitz and Thomas J. Boyle alert the DCOM to potential sources of environment-related trouble and describe how the data center environment can be properly controlled.

1 Developing Organizational Efficiency

by Philip C. Cross

INTRODUCTION

An organization cannot function successfully over an extended period of time without being able to change and adapt to outside influences. People come and go or transfer within the organization. Technology and scope of services become more complex and diversified. An organization cannot deal with these changes haphazardly; rather, it must confront them in a consistent, organized manner.

Many managers, unfortunately, do not recognize this fact. They focus on managing the entities within the organization rather than the organization itself. They direct attention to detail rather than provide the framework, facilities, and other necessary environmental conditions needed by people to do their jobs. This approach is frequently adopted by data center operations managers (DCOMs) because of the amount of effort they usually devote to daily operational problems. The DCOM should instead attempt to relate problem solutions to both short- and long-term conditions. The DCOM will find this difficult, however, unless he understands all the aspects of organization management.

This chapter discusses several organizational management techniques that the DCOM can practice. Most of the methods are straightforward and have been successful in well-managed data centers.

ORGANIZATIONAL STRUCTURE

If someone is asked to explain the organizational structure within which he works, he usually begins by drawing a diagram like the one shown in Figure 1-1. The boxes represent functional areas of responsibility and groups of people supervised by managers. The hierarchy of the boxes represents levels of authority; that is, the boxes higher on the chart represent greater authority. The lines between the boxes indicate the chains of command.

Such a chart conveys a great deal of information. It portrays an organizational framework and thereby provides management control. Charts, however, merely illustrate how things are supposed to be rather than how they really are.

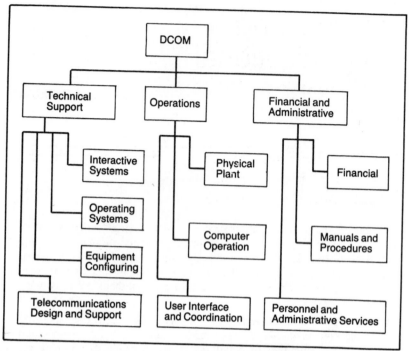

Figure 1-1. Data Center Organization Chart

Effective organizations do not just happen. Organization structure can be superficial and meaningless unless its two important components, people and functions, are properly arranged and interrelated.

The Black Box Concept

The concept of functional organization involves the process of breaking down all activities to the task level. Tasks are then treated as "black boxes," each with inputs and outputs (see Figure 1-2).

Structuring at the task level relates tasks both to and between people by portraying relationships among tasks that can easily be related to job positions. As task boxes emerge, they are assigned to people, producing a second level of boxes. While the task box level involves single tasks, the people box level involves multiple tasks. The constraints that must be kept in mind, however, when matching tasks to people are:
- The number of tasks a person can perform
- The complexity of the tasks
- The interdependencies among tasks

As people boxes are constructed for the entire data center, clusters emerge as work center boxes. As is the case for task and people boxes, work center boxes will indicate lines of dependence. At this point, the work center boxes

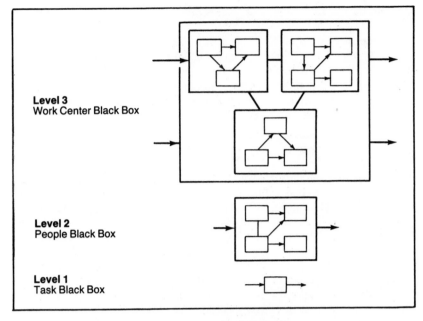

Figure 1-2. Black Box Hierarchy

could become the boxes shown in Figure 1-1 or could evolve into another level, depending on the complexity and scope of the individual data center.

Perceived versus Real Influences

Once an organizational structure has been identified, it serves as a framework for management and control. It may, however, stop short of truly identifying the personality of the organization in terms of subliminal spheres of influence. This is because levels of authority, as perceived through implied or defined supervisory status, do not take into account power centers stemming from personalities or the suggestive (or direct) influence that some job positions (even nonsupervisory ones) exert. As a result, the DCOM may be unaware of areas of conflict.

Although the DCOM may prefer to let lower-level supervisors deal with such problems as part of their job, he really cannot afford to take this attitude. To do so would be to ignore the subliminal power structure in the data center and the difficulties subordinate managers have in dealing with it. The fact is that the DCOM must assume the responsibility for subordinating managers to his own experience and management overview and must supervise their overall performance to help them cope with problems that they may not be able to handle. In order to assume this responsibility, the DCOM must understand how the data center really works in both an overt and covert sense. Once such knowledge has been acquired, the DCOM can work with subordinate managers to eliminate problems and contradictions, thus bringing perceived relationships into harmony with actual relationships.

Organizing Data Center Management

As emphasized earlier, the organization is only a starting point. It provides a frame of reference and must be appropriate for the functions to be performed and the work to be accomplished. It is not an end in itself. Once the organization is established and the DCOM is intimately familiar with the functional and personnel elements that comprise the organization, the DCOM must coordinate all of these elements to maximize organizational efficiency.

The following analyses concentrate on those areas that warrant the most emphasis to maximize organizational results.

Leadership. The DCOM exerts more influence on data center personnel than does any other person. For example, the behavior of the DCOM tends to be imitated by subordinates who report directly to him. The DCOM, therefore, must promote a style that is desirable for emulation. This should not be limited merely to demeanor and appearance. The DCOM must act in a way that projects an image of professional commitment to efficiency.

Management Meetings. If the DCOM and subordinate managers are to set the attitude and pace for the data center, it follows that they must unite in their thinking and actions. If they do not, they will tend to fragment, rather than combine, talents and energies that should be geared toward achieving the goals and objectives of the data center.

Such a management team, however, should not be limited to the DCOM and immediate supervisors. It should also include lower levels of management. A successful method of promoting team effort is to hold regularly scheduled management meetings chaired by the DCOM. The meetings need not be as frequent as the meetings between the DCOM and immediately subordinate managers. Whereas senior data center manager meetings would be held three or four times a month, general management meetings would be held once a month. Because all managers throughout the data center regard the DCOM as their leader, they should feel that they are members of the management team. They can achieve this sense of integration by attending meetings chaired by the DCOM.

The DCOM who does not recognize this need is likely to foster within the data center isolated groups in which each of the DCOM's subordinate managers communicates only with his or her subordinates. Meetings with different levels of management can also provide the DCOM with an insight into the attitudes and abilities of junior managers.

Disclosing Information. How much information should a DCOM disclose to subordinate managers? The DCOM is frequently privy to details that should not be related to subordinates. This confidentiality is not necessarily because the information threatens the job security of subordinates or the stability of the data center; rather, it is because such information might be perceived as threatening if it is not filtered carefully and conveyed in the proper context under the right conditions.

The DCOM must determine who should know what and ensure that information travels accordingly. When sharing information with subordinates, however, the DCOM takes care to not become characterized as a teller of half-truths who is involved in some kind of manipulative management game.

Technical Interface. As the complexity and scope of DP continue to expand in business, technicians must provide information to upper management. Technical input is exerting an increasingly significant influence on company DP management decisions and planning.

The DCOM functions as a middleman in the flow of information between technicians and company management. The most difficult aspect of this role for the DCOM is the probability of being caught in between (i.e., between upper management, who suspects and perhaps resents that DP technicians overly influence business decisions, and the technicians, who believe they must tell upper management what must be done). In these conditions, the DCOM must promote a sense of objectivity for both factions and dispel any distrust and resentment. The DCOM can accomplish this by having upper management request pertinent studies and special projects that demonstrate to the technicians that upper management understands current and future problems and needs and depends on the technicians to provide information for decision making. During this process, the DCOM must create an environment in which upper management does not perceive itself as being steered by the technicians, and the technicians see themselves as not the masterminds behind DP management decisions but as valuable company resources employed by management.

Bypassing. Bypassing lower-level managers and dealing directly with their subordinates can be considered a privilege of rank. Is this practice warranted to the degree that some DCOMs exercise it?

If bypassing is done frequently, the person contacted by the DCOM can easily lose sight of his immediate superior, the supervisor who must be satisfied. The DCOM obviously has authority over the entire data center, but the immediate superior is the one who assigns work, sets the daily working environment, and rates employee performance.

Frequent bypassing can affect both the manager and the subordinate. The subordinate may wonder about his manager's credibility with the DCOM. The subordinate may focus on self-centered strategies in order to gain favor with the DCOM, rather than devote attention to assignments given to him by the manager. The manager, in turn, may wonder about his job position and the possible motives of the DCOM.

A DCOM given to this type of behavior should determine why he acts this way. If it is because the manager is incompetent, that manager should be replaced. If the DCOM is too impatient, he must constrain that trait. In any event, managerial leadership is the ability to get things done through people, not around or in spite of them (especially not within one's own reporting chain). Efficiency can best be attained jointly by the DCOM and subordinate managers, with everyone doing his part without management intervention.

Delegating Authority. If the data center organization chart shows all functional responsibilities throughout the center, as well as the job positions related to those responsibilities, the chart has effectively designated specific spheres of authority. The chart becomes meaningless, however, if the DCOM does not delegate that authority.

Defining authority is, perhaps, the easiest part of delegating it; the more difficult aspects are determining that the person charged with the responsibility can properly exercise it and ensuring that everyone recognizes the authority and cooperates with the person charged with it.

Taxing High Performers. It is easy for a DCOM to overload more proficient personnel. For the high performers, the result can be demoralizing because they must work longer hours than their coworkers, but because of the demands placed on them, they may not be able to perform their assignments to their own satisfaction. The low performers may slacken even more because they are not given assignments that develop and challenge them and because they cannot learn from the high performers because those people cannot afford to spend time with them. The consequences are that overall data center performance steadily deteriorates, and the center tends increasingly to depend on only a few key people.

Making Work. The demand that senior data center managers place on subordinate personnel for data, reports, and justifications is often taken for granted by those managers as a necessary part of data center operation resulting from the center's complexity, service performance demands, and high cost of operation. But how much data is really needed, and how much manpower is exhausted in obtaining it? What line assignments are neglected? These questions must be seriously considered by the DCOM; data gathering and deciphering and report generation can become major drains on data center personnel.

Wall charts, tables, graphs, and computer listings can be valuable data center management tools. Some are worth the effort required to maintain them; others are not. The DCOM cannot afford to believe that juggling, rearranging, and manipulating statistics are panaceas for management and control. Data center managers who believe this are usually seeking to avoid making decisions and taking direct action to attain and maintain organizational efficiency. Indiscriminate accumulation of data can easily cause confusion and indecision, not to mention frustration among subordinates who must perform statistical and bookkeeping routines that they were not hired to do.

Working for Subordinates. Unfortunately, many managers regard leadership as confined to a very narrow set of duties that exclude the responsibility to provide productive working conditions for subordinate personnel. Setting goals and objectives, creating and maintaining an effective organization, paying salaries commensurate with performance, and providing training and education are a few of the ways that a manager works for subordinates. Mediocre performance and poor attitudes can usually be traced to management insensitivity to the needs of subordinates or to the demands imposed on them.

Status reporting, for example, is an excellent means for subordinates to identify areas where they need help from upper management. Many managers, consequently, ignore status reporting because they do not want their subordinates to "build fires" under them. Another example is the lack of managerial concern over inadequate furniture and less than ideal office conditions. When these conditions exist, subordinates are justified in believing that management is not interested in helping or motivating them. A DCOM cannot expect subordinates to perform when they know that the DCOM can change these conditions but apparently will not be bothered.

Making Decisions. Decisions must be made in data centers every day. Some decisions require immediate and decisive action, while others must be made over a longer term.

To a great extent, the timeliness and correctness of decisions depend on the capability and knowledge of the manager. If the manager is well informed, chances are that the decision will be correct and will accomplish the desired result. If the manager relies on chance when weighing alternatives, the probability of a correct decision diminishes.

Good decisions result in respect for the decision maker as well as confidence in him and the decision-making process. The DCOM, therefore, should provide senior management with all information and counseling necessary for making clear and timely decisions that are beyond the DCOM's authority.

Administrative versus Technical. A DCOM cannot be the chief technician in the data center. That responsibility lies with subordinate personnel. Those subordinates should not lose sight of the managerial viewpoint just as the DCOM must have some technical insight and understanding. This balance of information should be distributed throughout the data center, as indicated in Figure 1-3. This linear distribution is ideal because it assumes that proportionate relationships exist throughout all job positions and that the DCOM can rely on lower levels for the proper managerial and technical balance. In such an environment the DCOM must have some technical expertise, but not to the point where he loses sight of management objectives. If such shortsightedness occurs at the DCOM level, it will prevail throughout the entire organization, resulting in imbalances at all levels.

Productivity. Conveying a sense of urgency to personnel to get them to increase their productivity is a technique that must occasionally be employed by the DCOM. It should be used during peak processing periods, during hardware and software installations, to solve critical operating problems, to meet important project deadlines, and in other unusual circumstances.

The degree to which this technique is effective depends on how often it is used. Subordinate personnel usually rise to the occasion when they recognize that the need exists. If increased productivity is needed because of poor

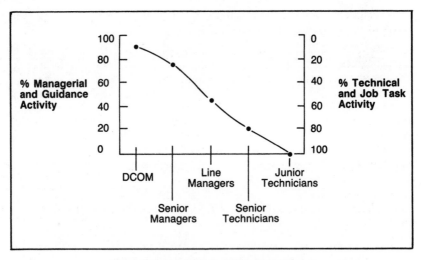

Figure 1-3. Technical vs. Managerial Input

management, personnel will resent having to make an extra effort that could have been avoided if:

- Planning had been better
- Priorities had been better set
- Staffing and budget were adequate
- Support from other groups were provided
- Deadlines were realistic
- Job responsibilities were clear
- Organizational conflicts were eliminated

These activities are the responsibility of management—if not to do, at least to ensure that they are done. The DCOM, therefore, must ensure that the sense of urgency is not caused by managerial ineptitude.

SETTING PRIORITIES

A data center that must meet high service requirements, yet keep costs down, must set its priorities very carefully. Some priorities, of course, are established by daily circumstances. This type of priority setting, often labeled reactive management, cannot be avoided totally because of the on-demand nature of DP and the external events that are likely to occur. When this mode of operation becomes a way of life, however, and consumes most of the effort and attention of data center managers and their subordinates, it indicates that very little attention is being given to at least minimizing a crisis environment.

There are many approaches to effective priority setting in a data center. Problems, of course, will occur that must be addressed immediately, and they should be a first-level priority. Second-level-priority problems would be those events that need not be addressed immediately but in the very near future. Such events are typically one-time problem-solving projects. Third-level-priority problems also take the form of one-time projects—those that enhance operational ability and prepare for expansion of service and technology, without a great deal of preliminary work.

This priority hierarchy is self-evident and will naturally occur in a data center. The lesson to be learned, however, is that although first-level priorities are mandatory, they should not be the only problems addressed. If they are, data center services will rapidly deteriorate.

Goals and Objectives

In order to set priorities, the DCOM must understand the goals of the data center. Those goals must be consistent both with the goals of the department within which the data center resides and with those of the company. If they are not, then the data center's goals could become counterproductive. For example, there is always a trade-off between service performance and the cost of providing those services. A data center can provide outstanding services (e.g., fast response and turnaround times) if there are no restrictions on the money provided for that purpose. Austere expense limitations, however, may restrict the DCOM's ability to attract and retain high-level technicians, obtain and support required operating software packages, perform accurate hardware analyses, and apply tuning improvements to enable the DCOM to produce that extra 10 to 20 percent utilization. Because such activities can avoid or postpone equipment upgrades, such limitations become penny-wise and pound-foolish.

Another situation in which goals may become confused is when a data center is accountable on a profit-and-loss basis. Such a center may regard its ultimate objective as breaking even and may, therefore, concentrate its attention on high-revenue users at the expense of lower-revenue producers. This view could contradict the company goal to maximize income should the smaller DP user have a greater impact on company income than the larger user and need DP services to obtain that income.

It is important, therefore, that the DCOM make certain that all data center goals and objectives support company goals and objectives. Any differences of opinion, at any personnel level, should be resolved and made to conform to management policy.

Frequently, however, this does not occur because the DCOM assumes that everyone understands the data center's goals and objectives. Although data center personnel usually understand that the goal of the data center is to provide maximum service at lowest cost, they do not always recognize inherent trade-offs between cost and service objectives. Unless these trade-offs are defined by the DCOM and properly understood, there is little chance that either set of objectives will be satisfied. The DCOM may, however, purposely avoid precise definition of goals and objectives for fear they may be misinterpreted. For example, management emphasis on reducing expenses can be misinterpreted by employees as lower merit increases, reductions in training and development, and fewer facilities, thus leading employees to resign or develop poor attitudes toward the company.

Planning

Defining goals and objectives paves the way for planning. Plans should identify both the tasks and the activities required to achieve those goals and objectives as well as the necessary resources (i.e., people, money, and facilities).

To facilitate planning and subsequent tracking against plan, project/goal sheets must be prepared. Depending on the scope of the goals and the projects required to accomplish them, there can be many projects for each goal. For identification purposes, numbers should be assigned to each goal and to the projects for each goal (e.g., the goal "reduce operating expenses" could have such projects as reducing equipment costs, reducing overtime, reducing supplies, and selling printout scrap). The numbering for this example might be:

Reduce operating expenses	1.00
Reduce equipment costs	1.01
Reduce overtime	1.02
Reduce supplies	1.03
Sell printout scrap	1.04

This simple numbering scheme would serve as the basis for project management and control. The project/goal sheets would also include time schedules and the resource requirements needed to accomplish the project.

A summary sheet could then be prepared periodically to show cumulative planned versus actual resource expenditures and milestones (results) by project.

Identifying resource requirements in this manner provides a means for unifying and maximizing all resources in the data center and can be extended to include resources contributed by departments outside the center.

Project Management and Control

The foregoing method of planning also facilitates tracking, an important element in effective project management. The numbering scheme can be extended to include identifiers for the functional areas in the data center. For example, project 1.01, reduce equipment costs, might be assigned to the technical support center, which could have an identifier of 3. The number for this project would then be 1.013. In this way, the key functional work center is tied to the project number and to the goal achievement of the data center. Consequently, status reporting and tracking are possible on a project level and on a goal level. This method, although simple, is valuable if it is not allowed to grow out of proportion through voluminous and irrelevant data and reports.

Project management cannot be limited to one-time projects; it must also include on-going activities. One such activity is keeping operating software up to date; another is maintaining telecommunications installations; still another is issuing trouble reports. Ongoing activities such as these should be regarded as projects, assigned identification numbers, quantified as to the effort expended on them, and keyed to the data center goals so that neither their importance nor the resources spent on them are ignored.

Status Reporting

Managers often become so involved with status reporting and project control that they defeat the efficiencies they are promoting. This usually happens in one of two ways:

- The manager may not understand the work being performed and/or have no confidence in the people performing it. The manager may, consequently, believe that frequent and complex status reports will make subordinates more productive because they are held in a position of detailed accountability.
- The manager may understand what is going on but may not know how to establish realistic measurements to track and control the project without detailed reports.

The secret of successful status reporting is a method that permits the project manager and subordinates to take timely and constructive action when it is needed.

The primary reason for status reporting is to alert project workers before disaster strikes. This can be done without voluminous reporting; adhering to milestones usually suffices. This approach requires the DCOM to have confidence in subordinates' ability to perform and progress satisfactorily between checkpoints without detailed status reporting. This confidence comes from the DCOM's comprehension of the functions performed by subordinates, the capabilities of the people performing them, and the relationships within the data center and with outside support groups. A direct correlation usually exists between this level of knowledge and the ability to successfully administer both ongoing and one-time projects with available resources. The DCOM also has a better relationship with upper management because he is in a better position to prevent subordinates from drowning in more work than they can complete and from having to cope with problems over which they may have no control.

Management of Time

Just because everyone in the data center is busy and works long hours does not mean that their time is used as efficiently as possible. If an average employee in a data center repeatedly comes in early, works through the greater part of the lunch hour, and stays late, something is definitely wrong, either in the way the people are managed or in the way they manage their own work activities. This particular situation is frequently attributed to too much work, the result of understaffing. The underlying cause can usually be traced to poor project identification and management priorities. Effective priority setting and project management usually result in more effective use of resources.

The proper work situation is exemplified by personnel reporting to work 15 to 20 minutes before starting time, being punctual on lunch breaks, and staying beyond quitting time an average of 15 to 20 minutes. Generally the DCOM who manages time effectively sets the example for the data center.

MAXIMIZING PERSONNEL EFFECTIVENESS

A DCOM can be compared with a ship captain, steering the best course possible to reach a destination. While underway, the captain must inspire the crew to keep the ship working well and to manage any unusual or threatening conditions that may occur.

Assignment and Work Load

As noted, each data center member must understand his work assignment and how it relates to the data center goals. The work load assigned to him should be within his performance capability. The project/goal charts described earlier facilitate appropriate work assignments, both at the individual and at the group levels.

Performance

Once the framework is established, it is necessary to appraise performance at these levels. Project milestones function as measurement standards. Periodic appraisal in relation to project milestones and services levels provides indicators of personnel efficiency and identifies training and education requirements for further performance improvements.

Performance appraisal, in this regard, is not intended as the basis for merit review and salary increase but as the basis for developing the individual as a valuable resource for the data center and, therefore, for the company.

Policies and Procedures

Ensuring that the assignments and the work loads related to those assignments are commensurate with the employee's abilities can increase efficiency. Policies and procedures are needed, however, if data center personnel are to perform well consistently and attain corporate goals.

From a hierarchical standpoint, policies can be regarded as rules and regulations needed to enforce the data center's goals. The procedures provide the methodology needed to ensure that those policies are enforced in a predetermined manner, particularly at lower-level positions where individual initiative is limited and in areas where the nature and structure of the organization (or perhaps the personalities involved) require that tasks be performed in a very specific way.

There are times when adherence to procedures is so important that the DCOM and senior management must approve them for enforcement and compliance. Some procedures are administrative in nature; others are production oriented. Examples of the former are purchase order approval and cost justification; examples of the latter are master terminal operation, tape retrieval, and backup and restore. No matter what they entail, these procedures must be viewed as a vital link between desired performance and data center goals.

The DCOM must be careful to ensure that procedures do not become complex and confusing and that they remain pertinent, clear, concise, and current. Procedures can be less burdensome if a training and education program for personnel is established. This program might use the set of written procedures as references, allowing personnel to assimilate procedures as part of their formal training rather than forcing them to interpret them on the job, where the result could easily be erroneous application.

Some of the dangers of generating too many procedures are as follows:

- People do not always pay attention to methods and procedures (perhaps because they are inaccurate or incomplete, are not given to those who need them, are too complex, or are not enforced).
- There are too many forms to be completed (perhaps because no one takes the time to audit existing procedures or the information that must be captured is not really necessary).
- Captions on forms do not apply (perhaps because sufficient explanation has not been provided or the forms have not been updated with changes that have occured in procedures or in the organization).
- Disagreement frequently occurs about the necessity of a procedure (perhaps because no one can relate it to a data center goal).
- Forms are frequently sent to the wrong people after they are completed or are returned to the originator because they do not contain the proper information (perhaps because the procedures are inadequate).
- Delays in projects can be traced to bottlenecks created by forms (perhaps because forms are not completed properly, not taken seriously, or delayed because they are time-consuming).
- The methods and procedures department has become an end in itself (perhaps because it tends to exert more control over functional departments than is advisable).
- Committees are continually reviewing existing procedures and recommending new ones (perhaps because such committees are self-perpetuating and have no specific, task-oriented goals).
- Procedures are keyed to politically oriented policies and are therefore a vehicle for regulating rather than guiding (perhaps because the nature of the activities being performed must be controlled or restricted).
- No clear definition exists between high- and low-level priority procedures (perhaps because the procedure writers are not aware of those priorities).

Another sign of bureaucracy is "memoitis," the practice of writing memos about anything and everything. The greatest danger is that such memos can become a substitute for personal contact in a dynamic organization. Memos are a necessary part of business activities in a data center (i.e., to issue directives, confirm agreements and actions, or for general communication). They are only one part of the communication process, however; overuse decreases their effectiveness. They are not a substitute for concise, clear, and well-conceived policies and procedures that must be institutionalized throughout the organization.

STRATEGIES

No department within a company, nor a company itself, can afford not to have a long- and short-term organizational strategy. Such strategy permits development to occur smoothly and effectively and is the basis for growth and stability. There is no such thing as a static organization. The market, financial considerations, and people change; with that change comes a need to adapt.

Adapting to Change

To adapt the data center to change, a DCOM must have a complete understanding of:
- Current staff capabilities
- Jobs and tasks being performed
- Short- and long-term plans and goals of the departments and the data center
- Requirements for accomplishing those goals

Once the DCOM understands these prerequisites, he should then know the current status of the data center, what the center should accomplish within a defined period of time, and the requirements to meet that goal. If, in addition, there is a built-in flexibility and adaptability within the data center, most unforeseen events or changes can be readily absorbed with minimal impact on the center and its staff.

Anticipating Change

What is the probability of change? Is it correct for a DCOM to assume that because the data center has operated at a certain level for the past five years, it will continue to do so in the future?

In most data centers, such a static condition is unlikely because of the effects of technological change, increasingly favorable trends in the computer price/performance ratio, new storage and telecommunications breakthroughs, and greater numbers of packaged application systems. The DCOM who ignores these factors may one day find it impossible to adapt without experiencing a major and disruptive impact on the center.

Reorganization

Successful reorganizations don't just happen; they are the result of considerable planning and conditioning and are smoothly coordinated. In some cases, a reorganization is so smooth that the parties involved are not even aware that it is happening.

Reorganizing is sometimes viewed as a panacea for correcting many management problems, but reorganization can obscure or exaggerate the real issues. This is not to imply that reorganization is not a viable approach to solving management problems and adapting to change, but it does mean that reorganization, as an alternative to attacking basic management problems, must be carefully scrutinized to make certain that it is the solution to the basic problem. If the DCOM has followed the prerequisites identified earlier and reorganization appears to be the answer, then, by all means, it should be undertaken.

As the term implies, reorganization introduces change into the structure and operation of the data center. For this reason, it is sometimes avoided or used only as a last resort. In its extreme forms, it means a major reorganization of the company. In a moderate form, it means little more than a reassignment of duties among a few people or work centers. Even in its moderate form, reorganization cannot be performed rashly. It is precisely for this reason that an organizational strategy is mandatory.

CONCLUSION

Developing organizational efficiency and maximizing data center productivity require that the DCOM effectively manage his staff as well as their work environment. To manage the work environment effectively, the DCOM must:

- Minimize crisis management by establishing realistic goals and objectives, identifying important tasks and activities, and installing a project management and reporting system to track the progress of tasks and activities
- Maximize personnel effectiveness by carefully assigning tasks and activities and by establishing policies and procedures to aid data center personnel in fulfilling their assignments
- Develop both short- and long-range strategies to deal with change.

2 Career Planning in Operations
by Dr. William A. Hansen

INTRODUCTION

Anyone who has been in the DP industry more than a few years has witnessed substantial changes. Many people remember when the operations department was only a huge room filled with EAM equipment. The author of this chapter entered DP in time to see the last of the IBM 1401s and the first of the System/360s. The System/370 generation has reached maturity; in fact, some DP experts argue that this system is now suffering from advanced old age. Card systems have given way to tape, and tape has given way to disk. Mass storage, online systems, teleprocessing networks, and data bases have expanded the capabilities of new systems and the way in which systems are perceived by users.

These innovations have affected the capabilities of systems as well as the people in the systems and programming departments. Specialized jobs have been created, including data base administration and teleprocessing specialization. Instead of requiring only one systems programmer, which was sufficient in the past, most medium-sized shops now require one programmer for the control program, another for the access methods, another for the job entry subsystem, another for the telecommunications software, another for the data base software, and several more staff members for the software that comprises a complete operating system. In larger shops, a team of people is required for each of these functions.

Although there has been a tremendous growth of career opportunities in systems and programming, nothing much has changed in the area of operations, except the equipment. Many, if not most, operations departments have the same job descriptions and organizational structures as those developed 10 years ago. This lack of organizational change has both institutionalized old problems and introduced some new ones. This chapter describes resultant problems and offers the data center operations manager (DCOM) several suggestions for facilitating the future growth of data center operations personnel.

JOB STATUS IN OPERATIONS

Major differences have always existed between the job requirements for programmers and those for operators. Although most early programmers were former users, it soon became evident that programming is a skill requiring special training. Today, most companies require that programmer applicants have either a degree, training, or previous experience in DP. Companies with internal training departments will accept a college degree in such related fields as mathematics or business.

Programmers have received considerable attention in recent years. Their education, career paths, organization, management, certification, and psychology have been the focus of numerous articles and books.

The growing need for skilled programmers has increased salaries and introduced job opportunities; increased specialization has created jobs that did not exist 10 years ago. The programmer/analyst has been replaced by a coder, librarian, programmer, technical designer, team leader, analyst, data base administrator, and several other personnel. Although this diversification may have been caused by a search for greater productivity, the result has been more jobs, more money, and greater opportunities for advancement.

Underlining this trend is the recent controversy as to whether programmers should be considered professional, with the same status as physicians, lawyers, and certified public accountants. As was recently stated in an issue of *Computerworld*, however, ". . .no one has seriously asserted that status for operators."[1]

A Problem of Challenge

Why are operations personnel treated differently? Originally, when programming was recognized as an intellectual activity, computer operations consisted of a series of manual procedures: placing cards in a reader, mounting the correct forms in the printer, hanging a couple of tapes, and pressing the correct button. Operators (usually male) were also required to type a command to keep jobs running. This process describes the operator's job 15 years ago.

Because changes occurred gradually in operations, operators were able to adapt without difficulty. Few people outside operations, however, including many managers within operations, even noticed these changes. These people continued to view operators as glorified button-pushers.

Although some operators still load cards, change paper, and hang tapes, these are now minor aspects of their job. Online systems, less expensive direct-access devices, teleprocessing, micrographics, mass storage devices, and other innovations are reducing the amount of time the operator must devote to hardware. Approximately 90 percent of the operator's time is now involved with software, including entering commands, responding to messages, and, most important, checking the status of each system component in order to maximize the overall efficiency of the system.

The antiquated perception of the operator's job is thus responsible for the lack of change in those areas where the job draws from the environment. Operations personnel are still hired from vocational ranks. Many new operators were clerks in user departments or were data entry operators. Some are graduates of technical schools or junior colleges, where they were trained on secondhand equipment. Most are hired with little or no experience and are expected to learn on the job.

Salaries have not increased anywhere near the rate of those for programmers, despite a much higher turnover rate in operations and an equally critical need for skilled people. Good operators are hard to keep. The most qualified operators seek employment in large, innovative companies that offer salaries comparable to those for programmers.

Many operators are dissatisfied because of the lack of opportunities for advancement. While a programmer can expect a promotion to project leader, analyst, or systems designer, most operators are forced to remain in the same positions they reached after a few years' experience. Career planning has not developed beyond the traditional path from Operator C to Operator B to Operator A.

Some operators seek programming jobs as an escape because programming is seen as a path toward career advancement in terms of salary, opportunity, and respect. Although both programming and operations may be very technical positions, the skills needed by operators and programmers completely differ.

Evaluating Operations Work

A recent survey by J. Daniel Couger and Robert A. Zawacki indicates that "the people in operations consider themselves on the bottom of the totem pole."[2] Although this fact has been acknowledged for some time, the survey also suggests the reasons. Computer operators, data entry personnel, and data control personnel rated their jobs significantly below those of people in other occupations in four of five key characteristics and in two of three job motivators. On the average, operations personnel believe that their jobs lack variety, that they receive little feedback on their performance, that they have little responsibility, and that they lack a sense of "task identity" because they rarely see more than a small part of a complete application. The only areas in which operations personnel rated their jobs near the normal ratings for other jobs were in "task significance" and "job meaningfulness." Although their ratings for these job characteristics were still lower than those of people in other jobs, their response indicates that operations personnel do believe their jobs have some value to the company. An operator once confided that the message an operator usually receives is, "Your job is important, you are not."

Couger and Zawacki also compute an operator's job "motivating potential." Operations personnel and their supervisors ranked significantly lower than other workers, both white and blue collar, and especially lower than people in other DP jobs. Surprisingly, however, operations personnel are relatively satisfied with their jobs. Couger and Zawacki believe that most operators ''are not unhappy 'biding their time' in present jobs—in anticipation of promotion to better jobs.'' Employees can be satisfied ''by paying them well, keeping bosses off their backs, and arranging things so the days pass without undue stress or strain.'' In order to increase the job's motivating potential and thereby improve productivity, the job itself must be restructured. Couger and Zawacki recommend ''job enrichment'' and ''job enlargement.'' They offer a procedure for soliciting suggestions and following through on them but do not, unfortunately, offer any concrete suggestions on how the jobs should be restructured. This decision is left to individual installations.

Thomas Zillner reaches the same conclusions. He considers computer operations ''boring and rarely (offering) enough challenge to attract and/or retain fully qualified people from other jobs, leaving operations to less imaginative individuals.'' He recommends involving operations personnel in the early phases of system design to improve the documentation, job run characteristics, and error-handling procedures. He also offers suggestions to operators interested in career advancement within the field of operations, including taking advantage of educational opportunities, volunteering to improve system documentation, learning more about the installation's major applications, and joining professional organizations.

These recommendations do not, however, change the basic nature of the job from which good operators are fleeing. Again, a restructuring of the job is the essential requirement.

CHANGING JOB CONDITIONS

A DCOM has several options to select from in order to solve the problem of shortage of skilled people. Many organizations are trying to create more specialization and to identify new job functions. The few experienced personnel are designated master console operators; the rest of the system is run by unit record operators, tape pool operators, and disk pool operators.

This type of organization, unfortunately, suffers from some of the same problems facing operators. Unless there is a serious effort to cross-train personnel, lower-level operators will quickly become bored. In addition, no one has been trained to fill the position of master console operator.

It may appear that such an arrangement improves conditions for the master console operator; however, this usually is not the case. By giving the easy tasks to lower-level operators, the job tasks of the master console operator become even more repetitive. The increased specialization also reduces the operator's sense of task identity since he sees an even smaller part of the whole job. In addition, few installations increase the responsibilities of the senior operator when the lower-level tasks are removed.

In reality, the senior operator's job is also being limited by technological advances. Modern operating systems are assuming many of the decisions formerly made by the senior operator. In cases where the operating system still allows flexibility, many installations have transferred some responsibility from the operator to the systems programmer. For example, many installations now forbid the operator to alter the number of active partitions or initiators.

Recognizing Job Importance

What should be done? First it is essential to realize the importance of the operator's job. Although operators may not require as much training as other DP personnel, they are in a critical position. It is not uncommon for two or three operators to be in total control of equipment worth from $3 million to $10 million. One mistake can cost thousands of dollars in rental costs and reruns, aside from the effect that a down computer has on a nationwide network. While a careless programmer can cost the installation much in test time and debugging, a careless operator can bring the entire corporation to a halt with a misplaced elbow.

Operators are in a critical position for another reason. No other DP group (except possibly a few system programmers) has such free access to an organization's files and records. Data security packages (e.g., RACF, Secure, or ACF2) are adequate for protecting data sets from unauthorized access by means of a terminal; however, these security measures cannot prevent an operator from taking a company's most valuable data. (This was attempted by a lead operator who took a key master file and all backup copies from his company's tape library and held them for ransom. He was eventually apprehended by the police.)

Salary. The first step in improving the operator's job should be to ensure that salary levels for operations personnel are equivalent to those offered by other corporations. Talk to the operators to learn if any unnecessary job hassles can be eliminated. Eliminating employee dissatisfaction is an easy step and one that, according to the Couger-Zawacki survey, most installations have already taken.

Training. The next step is a commitment to training and career advancement. Make sure everyone is aware of all jobs that are available within operations and the skills needed for promotion to those positions. Salary ranges should be published, provided a higher salary can result from greater skill and more responsibility.

Offer support for employees who want to improve their skills. Most companies offer a tuition refund program so that employees can enroll in college classes in a job-related field. Advertise the DP department's policies regarding attendance at conferences and seminars and membership in professional organizations. If your personnel are routinely sent to attend various events, make sure all personnel understand how to apply and how delegates are chosen.

In-house training facilities can also be developed to improve employee skills. Employees can demonstrate certain skills as a prerequisite for promotion. Offer self-study and multimedia courses as a way of attaining these skills; however, the demonstration of skills should be used as the criterion for advancement rather than the completion of courses. This approach eliminates having to make an exception for new employees with previous experience and eliminates promotion for employees who merely "pass time" in a class. When selecting training materials, look for those that teach specific job skills rather than those that teach about a subject. The most motivated students are those who can see a clear relationship between mastering course objectives and success on the job.

If your organization has a full-time training manager, ask him to help create a formal skills inventory to determine what skills are required for each job function and what skills are actually possessed by staff personnel. This type of assistance can lead to a cost-effective method of staff training that permits staff participation in only the courses that address immediate skill requirements.

Each organization has its own training policy. Some require a mandatory number of training days per year for each job function; others train on a more sporadic basis. Employee motivation is the determining factor; it is very difficult to prevent a motivated employee from learning. If in-house training is unavailable, the operator may elect to read manuals at the console or enroll in courses after working hours. Thus, it is important that the employer provide materials to employees who want them. Paying people to take classes is always less successful than holding up a target (a required skill), passing out the arrows (training opportunities), and rewarding those who succeed (with a better job).

Management should not, however, be discouraged if some people fail to take the opportunity for additional training. These people might be sufficiently challenged by their existing jobs. If they are happy in their present environment and are performing their job tasks well, let them alone. They should not be forced into positions of greater responsibility if they show no desire to advance. Operators have quit rather than give up easy (albeit low-paying) jobs that they have mastered.

Publicizing career paths and making training available solves the career advancement problem until the employee reaches the senior positions within operations.

Application Identification

Couger and Zawacki state that a major problem with most current operations jobs is the lack of task identification. Usually, each operator sees only a portion of an application and does not understand how his contribution fits into the whole. Zillner recommends that operators desiring advancement make an effort to learn how each job they run actually works. For example, he recommends that an operator study the documentation to learn what happens as an input tape is processed to produce an output tape. Being able to knowledgeably discuss the applications being run is one way of building user and programmer confidence in the operator's abilities.

A broader knowledge of applications among operators can reduce errors and false starts and improve overall motivation while stressing general business goals of the organization.

Once this process is initiated, be prepared to develop a follow-up procedure. As soon as the operators are requested to learn about the jobs they are running, a formal procedure to identify and follow up on their suggestions will be needed. One easy way to develop a procedure is to modify the traditional trouble report to support suggestions and recommendations from the operations staff. If such a procedure is not implemented, numerous problems can develop.

The author once worked at an installation that used a traditional suggestion box but no follow-up procedures. An operator modified the production JCL for a job by moving the temporary data sets passed between steps from tape to disk. He went through proper channels and got a chance to demonstrate his changes to management. The job execution time dropped from 55 minutes to less than 5, primarily because of the removal of 24 tape mounts. The managers, however, concluded that there must be some reason the job had been so designed; after all, an analyst should know better than an operator. (In fact, the job was a carry-over from a time before disks were invented.) The operator continued to use his version of the JCL whenever he ran that job. He was soon fired for "exceeding his job description." The company lost a valuable employee, and the episode had further costly consequences. The operators who remained stopped making suggestions and started doing the minimum work required. In addition, the more skilled operators quietly looked for other jobs or applied for transfers to programming. The application existed in the same form for a couple more years. It was even converted when the company switched hardware vendors. A great amount of computer time and operator effort were lost. Years later, a maintenance programmer happened to find the job and made the recommended changes.

The moral of this story is obvious. Either provide a method for operators to make suggestions (and to have their suggestions implemented), or risk continued inefficiency, the loss of talented employees, and lack of motivation from those operators who remain.

Improving Group Interaction

This same installation also provides an example of productive operations/systems programming relations. Initially, DP personnel's contempt for the operations department was so intense that operations personnel had little input in matters that affected them directly. For example, during a major conversion, the programming department decided what run documentation it would provide to operations. This decision produced a flood of abends that could not be fixed by the operations staff. The reluctance of the programmers to respond to 3:00 A.M. telephone calls led to the creation of a technical support group within operations to diagnose and correct JCL problems, approve all run documentation, and write all production JCL.

A major shake-up at this installation was required to correct all problems. A new operations manager and systems programming manager guided operations through the conversion according to schedule. They were unaware that their predecessors had never communicated concerning their tasks. The failure of systems and programming to meet conversion dates convinced upper-level management to give operations a free hand. A completely new systems programming staff wrote a new users manual, ignoring the old standards written by the programming department.

The change was substantial. Operators helped set standards that were enforced by the systems programmers by means of operating system parameters. Operators requested and quickly received such job aids as console commands to list catalogs and data set labels. Operator morale as well as productivity increased significantly. The technical support group started working directly with users to improve scheduling and response time to problems.

Much of the improvement at this installation was a direct result of giving operators a greater voice in operational functions and establishing communication between operators and systems programmers. When operators noticed a problem and either asked for help or recommended a solution, the systems programmers responded. The fewer problems encountered, coupled with the increase in throughput, impressed on senior management the capabilities of both groups.

A PROPOSED CAREER PATH

Most installations now have a job known as technical support specialist, operations analyst, or scheduler. These people, who work within operations, are the first ones contacted when a production job terminates abnormally. Technical support specialists are allowed to fix JCL errors but must contact the appropriate programming personnel when a problem results from a programming error. At many installations, this group is also responsible for maintaining the production program library and the JCL procedure library. They often have the responsibility for writing or approving the JCL and running documentation for all production jobs. In some cases, technical specialists serve as the liaison between operations and the user departments, similar to the customer representatives in a service bureau. The position of technical specialist is a logical growth path for operators, especially for those who have made an effort to learn about the applications they are running.

Another logical growth path for the operator is the position of junior systems programmer. Many systems programmers have four-year degrees in computer science. Although this is a reasonable prerequisite for senior positions, it is not required for the tasks performed during the first few years on the job. In addition, at a junior level of programming, there is little need for extensive programming experience. Most junior systems programmers use utility programs or other parameter-driven systems. While the senior systems programmers make long-term plans (selecting equipment and software packages) or are involved with very technical work (performing system generations or modifying and tuning the operation system), the junior staff performs the more daily responsibilities. They monitor utilization and error reports, perform routine maintenance, and help the master console operator diagnose system-related problems. Senior operators could easily move into these positions. In addition to the direct benefits to them, this would also relieve the more technically trained specialists to move into the jobs requiring their skills.

Figure 2-1 illustrates a suggested career path for operations personnel. Note the planned path from senior operations positions to systems programming. Note, also, the distinction between professional and paraprofessional jobs. Many entry-level programming positions, like entry-level operations positions, are often filled by people with little or no DP experience or with just a two-year degree from a junior college or technical school. Senior master console operators, like senior programmers, require years of experience to master their jobs.

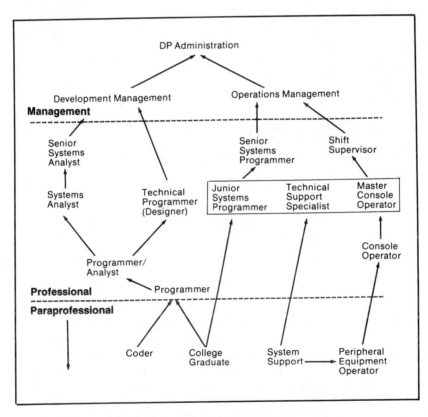

Figure 2-1. A Suggested Career Path Chart

Junior systems programmers, technical support specialists, and master console operators do not require knowledge of a programming language, although assembler programming is required for advancement to senior systems programming positions. All three jobs involve extensive interfacing with the operating system by means of operator commands, JCL, and utility control statements. Experience in any of these positions is advantageous for either of the other two. The skills acquired in these positions should be considered prerequisites for senior systems programming positions.

These three jobs—junior systems programmer, technical support specialist, and master console operator—should be placed at an equal level on organizational charts. Employees should be able to attain these positions by a number of career paths. Once there, they should be given the opportunity to rotate among these positions. By encouraging lateral job changes, managers can solve several problems simultaneously. Valuable employees who would otherwise leave because of the lack of advancement opportunity may remain. Cross-training can also increase overall productivity by increasing communication and decreasing the number of mistakes caused by lack of knowledge. In addition, cross-training can protect the installation against the loss of a key employee. By requiring cross-training in all three positions in order to receive a promotion to senior systems programming positions, the skill level in these jobs can be raised.

An installation may encounter several problems in implementing this plan. For example, an organization's definition of a professional employee may introduce problems for operators who must work overtime. The proposed career path, however, offers the opportunity for everyone to progress according to his ability. Very few people climb from the bottom to the top of an organization. Most reach their limits somewhere in the middle. Those who reach senior programming positions will do so only by demonstrating that they can assume the responsibility capably.

Another option is not obvious from the chart. It is possible to implement the plan by hiring only college graduates, on the way to systems programming, for all master console operator vacancies. This approach can bring the needed technical expertise to this job. Personnel who succeed in this position demonstrate they are very competent individuals who should be given an opportunity to move into more technical positions within the organization.

CONCLUSION

The following steps are suggested for improving the operator's job:
- Take care of basic job conditions first. Pay competitive salaries, and eliminate unnecessary job hassles.
- Define the skills that must be demonstrated for promotion to a particular position, and offer the training necessary.
- Encourage attendance at conferences, seminars, and professional meetings. Advertise tuition refund and internal training programs.
- Encourage operators to learn more about the jobs they are running and

to suggest ways of improving performance, and develop a procedure to follow through on their suggestions.

- Give operations personnel a greater voice in matters that affect them directly.
- Redesign jobs and career paths to provide greater opportunities within operations and systems programming.

Implementing these suggestions should reduce turnover, increase productivity, and help develop your most valuable resource—your personnel.

References

1. Zillner, Thomas. "Operator's Job Can Be Creative, Satisfying " *Computerworld* (June 4, 1979).
2. Couger, J. Daniel, and Zawacki, Robert A. "Something's Very Wrong With DP Operations Jobs." *Datamation* (March 1979).
3. Hansen, William A. "The Operator's Changing Status." *Datamation* (January 1979).

③ Data Center Documentation by Howard Schaeffer

INTRODUCTION

Well-defined and up-to-date documentation is necessary to ensure that a data center functions effectively, that systems can be understood, and that enhancements can be accommodated as needs change. Although the data center operations manager (DCOM) may question spending time and money on the preparation and maintenance of documentation when busy with more immediate problems (e.g., limited hardware and personnel resources, unpredictable user demands, hardware failures, abnormally terminated programs), these very problems are indications that documentation is needed. Without documentation, resource limitations and job rescheduling can cause frustration and destroy service reliability. Data center support for data communications especially requires good documentation; for example, without the proper reference materials, inappropriate or delayed response to console messages may disrupt dependent procedures and result in unexpected costs.

Such problems as scheduling, controlling batch job flow, and implementing contingency plans can be alleviated by well-defined methodology and accurate updating. Documentation can also aid in the periodic examination of jobs and their frequency of execution as well as in obtaining user cooperation in regulating the work load. In particular, documentation can provide the following benefits:

- Increased guidance for operations—A system with incomplete documentation may have been in production for weeks or even months when an unfamiliar and cryptic message appears on the console. The computer operator searches through the operator's manual but cannot find any reference to the message and has no idea what to do. After a flurry of calls to various analysts, programmers, and (if necessary) users, the answer may be supplied and the job completed. Even if user deadlines are not seriously affected, the incomplete documentation has disrupted operations and wasted time. Even more time may be wasted if the system documentation is also inadequate and the only sources of information are program listings. DP personnel naturally feel harried in such a situation, and users, especially those working at terminals, develop an unfavorable image of DP service.

- More maintainable systems—It is not unusual for the maintenance changes on a poorly documented system to create problems worse than those corrected. Often, systems personnel change the start-up, restart, or close-down procedures with only verbal communication to an operator, who, in turn, may not record this critical information in the operator's manual. Documentation must be adequate when a system goes into production and must be properly updated whenever a change is made. This procedure effects more rapid resolution of problems and, at the same time, helps avoid the creation of new ones.
- Easier enhancements—If a user requests additional control counts or a new report, the systems analyst or programmer needs accurate systems documentation to determine the point at which the new logic should be added. Without such records, much time is consumed for even the simplest enhancement. Good documentation can ease and speed up enhancements and can minimize the likelihood of creating new problems.
- Better training—Without documentation, the only means of providing DP procedures training for new personnel (whether computer operators, systems analysts, or users) is through personal instruction. The quality of this training depends on the completeness and accuracy of the instructor's knowledge and the limitations on the instructor's time. In addition, personal instruction without supporting documentation usually results in the trainee learning through frustrating and time-consuming trial and error.
- Improved user perspective—User management usually has only a general idea of what a system accomplishes. This minimal knowledge is inadequate for understanding why a system is troublesome or for evaluating system enhancements. Documentation provides the information management needs to determine whether to enhance a system or design an improved one. In addition, good documentation can result in improved employee morale and increased user faith in the DP system.

This chapter focuses on the documentation required in the data center. It provides guidelines for establishing documentation procedures, criteria for evaluating documentation, and methods for obtaining adherence to documentation standards. It also includes a detailed discussion of how to develop a user handbook. Sample procedures are included in the Appendix.

DOCUMENTATION REQUIRED IN A DATA CENTER

The types of documentation required in a data center can be classified according to their sources: the vendor, the systems development group, and the data center.

Vendor Documentation

Manuals must accompany all hardware that requires instructions for operation, correction of malfunctions, or judgment of compatibility with new hardware. Vendors should provide documentation for such hardware as consoles, tape and disk drives, and data communications monitors.

Software vendors must also provide manuals containing instructions for installing and using software, understanding error messages, and taking corrective action. Because systems programmers often work in the data center, it is also necessary that logic flowcharts and program coding be available for their use. Reference manuals should be available for such software as operating systems, utilities, tape library systems, job accounting systems, and the various performance-evaluation packages.

Obtaining vendor-prepared documentation is generally not a problem, although the quality of the documentation provided varies considerably.

Systems Development Documentation

Two sets of documents are required from the systems development group. The first, data preparation instructions, needs little discussion because comprehensive forms are generally used for data preparation. The format of these documents varies but must include field names and the record locations for the fields. The forms generally include such information as data type and editing criteria.

The second set of documents, operating instructions (often included in the operator's manual), is frequently inadequate. To be complete, it should include procedural information regarding response to error messages or abnormal program termination. For a batch system it is necessary to know if the correct execution of a program depends on satisfactory completion of preceding programs; for systems using data communications, it is necessary to know how to restart the system. Figures 3-1 and 3-2 are sample tables of contents for batch and data communications systems. Because data communications systems are new to many installations, the documentation in Figure 3-2 is discussed in detail. (The discussion of the first three sections also applies to documentation for batch systems.)

The first document in an operator's manual is the personnel contacts sheet, which provides a directory for rapid assistance should documented actions not resolve a problem. It contains each contact's name, responsibilities, department, and company (if they are not employees). Although this document often requires frequent updating, it is one of the most important in the manual.

The next document is the system summary. It provides a basic description of the system's overall purpose as well as its primary functional components and their relationships. It can also include statements on the system's benefits, present constraints, and potential changes. Figure 3-3 suggests how this information can be formatted. A functional chart of the system is prepared that displays the functional components and their relationships; each component is explained briefly in separate narrative sections.

The third section of the operator's manual contains a detailed flowchart of all programs, files, and online terminals. (For a batch system, the manual's

---

Operator's Manual—Accounting System

1. Personnel Contacts
2. System Summary
3. System Flowcharts
4. Hardware/Software Requirements
5. Scheduling Requirements
6. Input
   6.1   Tape/Disk
   6.2   Card/Paper Tapes
   6.3   Control and Parameter Cards
7. Processing
   7.1   Console Messages
   7.2   Balancing Instructions
8. Output
   8.1   Printer (including setup instructions and sample output)
   8.2   Computer Output Microfilm
   8.3   Tape/Disk
   8.4   Cards

Figure 3-1. Batch System Operator's Manual Table of Contents

Operator's Manual—Inventory System

1. Personnel Contacts
2. System Summary
3. System Flowcharts
4. Preprocessing
   4.1   Hardware Requirements
   4.2   Software Requirements
   4.3   Files Required
   4.4   Output Produced
   4.5   Scheduling Requirements
5. Processing
   5.1   Start-up Procedure
   5.2   Processing Controls
   5.3   Master Terminal Messages
   5.4   Master Console Messages
6. Postprocessing
   6.1   Close-down Procedure
   6.2   Offline Processing
7. Backup and Restart Procedures

Figure 3-2. Data Communications System Operator's Manual Table of Contents

system flowchart would show only the immediate program, the input and its sources, and the output and its destinations.)

The fourth section, preprocessing, describes necessary hardware and software resources, required input files, output formats, and scheduling requirements.

The fifth document details processing procedures and explains all status and exception messages that may be received. The sixth and seventh sections outline the procedures for close-down processing (completing all end-of-processing activities and verifying control counts), offline processing (e.g., initiating offline printing and offline preparation of microfiche), backup of critical files, and restart of processing with the backup files.

Two common problems are associated with systems development documentation. The first problem, actually procuring the documentation, can be eliminated by making the completion of these documents a prerequisite for accepting a system for production. The second problem, ensuring that the systems department updates documentation to correspond with system changes, is more difficult to solve. If documentation for version 5 of a system is being used when version 8 of the system is in production, processing will be inefficient and errors more frequent. A method of controlling this situation is to have the systems department state in writing that all affected documents have been updated after a system change or that no documentation update is

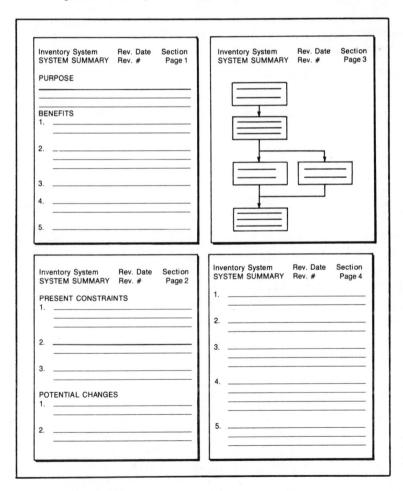

Figure 3-3. System Summary: Document Formats

necessary. If nothing else, this approach will protect operations from unfair criticism.

Data Center Documentation

Besides the processing logs for control, the flow and turnover of jobs, hardware problems, and so on, the two primary documents needed in a data center are a standards and procedures manual and a user handbook.

A suggested table of contents for a standards and procedures manual is provided in Figure 3-4. The actual decision as to what should be included and how the selected topics should be grouped depends on the situation. At some installations, systems department personnel perform hardware evaluation, relocation analysis, and performance evaluation; in such cases, performance standards and required procedures would not belong in the data center standards and procedures manual. Detailed guidelines for developing a user handbook are included in a later section of this chapter.

DOCUMENTATION CRITERIA

After the required documents are identified, documentation criteria must be established to guide documentation activities and to evaluate the results (see Figure 3-5).

Documentation criteria fall into two groups, those related to content and those governing format. In terms of content, documentation must be:
- Accurate
- Complete
- Clear
- Concise

Standards and Procedures Manual

1. Administrative Standards
    1.1   Organization Structure
    1.2   Job Descriptions
    1.3   Personnel Appraisal Procedure
    1.4   Budget Control
2. Operations
    2.1   Environmental Requirements
    2.2   Hardware and Software
    2.3   Work Flow and Controls
    2.4   Safety and Security
    2.5   Scheduling Methodology
    2.6   Tape Library System
    2.7   Job Accounting
    2.8   Contingency Plans
3. Support Services
    3.1   Site Layout and Data Center Relocation
    3.2   Hardware Selection Procedure
    3.3   Performance Evaluation
    3.4   Documentation Control

Figure 3-4. Standards and Procedures Manual Table of Contents

Type	Criterion	Basic Consideration
Content	1. Accuracy and 2. Completeness	Have at least two knowledgeable people reviewed the documentation?
	3. Clarity	Have at least two people unfamiliar with the documentation's subject matter reviewed it?
	4. Conciseness	Is the information shown really needed, and, if so, can it be entered on a form or presented in a chart?
Format	5. Ease of Reference	Is reference information located for quick reference?
	6. Ease of Use	Is information segmented and sequenced according to how information will be entered or referenced?
	7. Ease of Maintenance	Is information contained in small, independent units for easy updating or replacement?

Figure 3-5. Documentation Criteria

Accuracy and completeness can be appraised by personnel familiar with the system; clarity is best evaluated by people who may use the documentation but who are unfamiliar with the system. Conciseness can be checked by determining whether the information is actually needed and, if so, whether it can be presented more succinctly as a list or table. These criteria should be applied to each document produced.

The criteria related to format must only be applied when the format for a document is being standardized. The documentation format criteria are:
- Ease of reference
- Ease of use
- Ease of maintenance

The document's identification information must be easy to locate. For example, the section number on the procedure document shown in Figure 3-6 is conspicuously located. For ease of use, a document's contents should be segmented and sequenced in a practical manner. Thus, in the procedure document, all identification information is presented in the heading, then the general purpose of the procedure is stated, and finally the procedural steps are listed. Ease of maintenance is ensured by using modular documentation, permitting each unit to be easily updated or replaced.

THE USER HANDBOOK

A good user handbook minimizes the problems resulting from communication inefficiencies: unplanned or unrealistic demands on data center resources, uninvolved and uninformed users, and uncoordinated user/data center activities.

Unplanned or Unrealistic Demands on Data Center Resources. If the DCOM is unaware of new systems development or existing system modification, he or she will be unable to anticipate excessive demands on data center resources. Unanticipated demands also occur when the quantity of input for jobs increases significantly, particularly if keying and tabulating operations must be increased. Adequate forewarning can avoid demands that can only be met through such unsatisfactory methods as overtime for personnel or expensive purchase of off-site services. A vehicle for user/data center communication, such as a data center steering committee, is therefore necessary in order to anticipate and plan for all such demands. Whatever vehicle is chosen, the user handbook should formally document it and stress its importance.

The most expensive unplanned demands made on the data center involve job scheduling, in which users do not often participate. DCOMs, therefore, are unable to regulate the work load and minimize peak periods (when not all jobs can meet their deadlines) and slack periods (when the data center resources are not fully used). This situation becomes even more critical when unscheduled priority jobs occur frequently. Once standard procedure involving users is developed to resolve potential scheduling conflicts and to ensure efficient use of data center resources, the user handbook provides the documentation necessary for the DCOM to enforce that procedure.

Uninvolved and Uninformed Users. When users are neither involved in recommending processing improvements nor informed of processing problems, improved methods may be ignored and inefficiencies may continue. For

Procedure Documentation		
Procedure Title	**Rev. Date**	**Section**
Department	**Rev. No.**	**Page of**

    I.   **Purpose**

    II. **Procedure**

          Responsibility   **Activity**

          User   A.
                                  B.
          Scheduler   C.
          User   D.

    III. **Exhibits**

          A.
          B.

Figure 3-6. Format for Documenting Procedures

example, most users are unaware that incomplete input is sometimes submitted to the data center, requiring data center personnel to obtain the missing information. The problem may result from improperly designed forms or poorly trained user personnel. Whatever the cause, such problems waste time yet cannot be corrected unless users are notified of the situation. The user handbook can help ensure that correct input procedures are followed.

Another problem facing the DCOM is users who are receiving copies of reports they no longer need but have not instructed the data center to discontinue generating their copies. The user handbook can establish procedures to review requirements periodically and to determine whether all reports and copies are actually needed.

Users involved in improving efficiency in their departments and in the data center have the information necessary to enable them to consider such techniques as preparing input in the user department, online processing, and outputting onto microfiche instead of paper. These approaches can provide users with such benefits as increased control of their activities, faster service, and reduced processing costs.

Lack of Coordination between Users and Data Center. Poor coordination between users and the data center can impede the processing of a job at any time, from receipt for processing through the distribution of output. For example, if a scheduled job cannot be delivered to the data center on time, insufficient advance notice may eliminate the possibility of rescheduling the job to meet its deadline. A job may have been processed and rejects may have occurred; to get the corrected input processed on schedule, close user/data center cooperation is necessary. Even when a job is completed, arrangements must be made to distribute the output. The user handbook documents the methods of communication and coordination for all of these activities.

Goals of the User Handbook

The primary goal of the user handbook is to provide all procedures necessary to avoid the preceding problems and to promote increased cooperation and coordination between user and data center personnel (parts 2 and 3 in Figure 3-7); the procedures developed to satisfy this goal constitute most of the user handbook.

Two additional needs should also be satisfied: users should understand how the data center is structured and how it functions, and the DCOM should have a means for monitoring and enforcing adherence to the documented procedures (parts 1 and 4 in Figure 3-7). In addition, the user handbook should be prefaced by two statements, one describing its purpose and the other indicating upper management's approval and support. An optional addendum to the user handbook can supply the user with information for coordinating with systems development personnel; the addendum would explain how a project is initiated, how status reports are prepared, and how a system is accepted for production. Because projects are divided into a definite num-

Preface	The Purpose of the User Handbook	
Part 1	The Data Center Organization	
	1.1	Organization Chart
	1.2	Organization Components
	1.3	Processing Work Flow
	1.4	Processing Controls
	1.5	Safety and Security
Part 2	The Data Center Steering Committee	
Part 3	Procedures	
	3.1	Introduction to the Procedures
	3.2	Application Installation
	3.3	Application Maintenance
	3.4	Application Discontinuance
	3.5	Job Scheduling
	3.6	Unscheduled Jobs
	3.7	Data Submission
	3.8	Job Status Inquiry
	3.9	Error Correction
	3.10	Problem Resolution
Part 4	Adherence to Procedures	

Figure 3-7. Recommended Table of Contents for the User Handbook

ber of phases in most installations, users should know when each phase occurs and what involvement and responsibilities they have in each.

Contents

Preface. The preface states the primary goal of the user handbook—to guide and coordinate user and data center activities—and then lists the advantages of its use. It is important that users and data center management and staff regard the methods described in the handbook as standard procedures rather than recommendations for action. For reinforcement, the preface should include a statement of approval and support of the handbook from at least one higher-level manager to whom users and data center management report.

The Data Center Organization. The first part of the handbook informs users of the functions in the data center and how they are related. Section 1.1 presents a chart of data center functions, their relation, and the title of the person responsible for each. The chart should include such typical functions as data control, data preparation, scheduling, data center library, computer processing, and post-processing.

Section 1.2 briefly describes each of the functions, stressing areas in which users may be involved and the people (and their titles) with whom users may come into contact. Job flow through the data center is outlined in Section 1.3, and the processing controls for aiding timely and reliable processing of jobs are presented in Section 1.4. Of particular interest to users is Section 1.5, which describes the safety and security precautions taken in the data center.

The Data Center Steering Committee. Part 2 describes the data center steering committee, which guides and coordinates the activities of user and data center personnel. The committee's responsibilities include:

- Informing the DCOM of new systems development and existing systems modifications. This permits anticipation and preparation for increased demands on resources.
- Alerting the DCOM to sudden increases in input quantity, particularly if input requires keying or tabulating operations.
- Resolving scheduling conflicts that cannot be handled by users alone.
- Controlling the number of unscheduled jobs submitted to the data center.
- Notifying users of application inefficiencies and problems.
- Auditing the need for all reports, especially large ones, that users receive.
- Soliciting user ideas for improving efficiency, service, and control.
- Reviewing procedures for improving coordination between user and data center personnel.
- Obtaining adherence to procedures.

To be effective, this committee should not be too large, but it should include representatives of the data center and the major users. The committee reports regularly to upper management concerning its accomplishments and unresolved problems. It also can recommend increases in data center resources. The DCOM usually chairs the committee.

Procedures. Part 3 begins with an overview of the procedures, and Section 3.1 segments and explains them. The procedures shown in the table of contents under Part 3 can be divided into three categories: those related to applications (their installation, maintenance, and discontinuance), to job scheduling and data receipt, and to error correction and problem resolution.

The format recommended for documenting the procedures in Sections 3.2 through 3.10 is illustrated in Figure 3-6. A succinct statement of the purpose of the procedure is followed by the sequence of actions to be performed; each action identifies the person responsible for its execution. Each action direction should start with a command (e.g., deliver, enter, store). When reference is made to a form, report, or any other item that will be presented as an exhibit, it should be marked as such. The exhibits are then presented immediately after the procedure description. Further explanation of the exhibit can accompany the document itself, or the areas to be clarified can be keyed to a separate sheet of paper.

The procedures described in Sections 3.2 through 3.10 include all activities of user and data center personnel and clarify where each employee's responsibilities start and end. The details may vary according to an installation's structure and personnel. Some procedures shown may not apply for a particular DP installation; for example, user contact during application installation may be with the systems development department rather than with the data center. Conversely, some installations may require additional procedures (e.g., remote job entry, microfiche processing). Two sample procedures are outlined in the Appendix.

Adherence to Procedures. The final section explains how adherence to procedures will be monitored and enforced. Several monitoring methods can be used. One or more people can be assigned to monitor the effectiveness of and adherence to procedures and to report their findings to data center management. Alternatively, each workstation can report on its activities, using information contained in control logs. The monitoring method is documented in order to stress to personnel the importance of adhering to established procedures.

This section also prescribes the course of action to be adopted should an employee fail to follow these procedures. For example, it may state that a first-time irregularity will be corrected by the DCOM reviewing the reasons for the establishment of the procedures with the employee, while repeated violations by personnel outside the data center may be brought to the attention of the data center steering committee.

Preparation of the User Handbook

Preparation of a user handbook is very similar to preparation of any important report or publication, with a few additional steps. The team responsible for preparing the handbook is selected from user and data center personnel by the DCOM and should include at least one writer/editor. This team then proceeds according to the following instructions:

1. After a preliminary survey of what is involved, state the objectives to be obtained, and prepare a schedule. User and data center management should approve the statement of objectives and the schedule.
2. Collect information on procedures to be performed, data center functions and structures to be explained, and the necessary forms and reports.
3. Write a first draft to be reviewed for organization, completeness, and accuracy. Substance is more important than style at this stage.
4. Have the draft reviewed by data center and user personnel, and discuss comments to be sure they are understood.
5. Write a working draft that will include the discussed and approved changes. This draft should contain the substance of the final manuscript.
6. Obtain an editorial review of the working draft. This review will correct any deviations from the organization's style conventions (e.g., usage, grammar, spelling). In addition, suggestions may be made concerning the improvement of clarity and conciseness.
7. Write the final manuscript, considering all editorial recommendations. Check the typed manuscript for omission of material and typing errors.

8. Print the user handbook.

The data center and user personnel should then conduct orientation seminars and training sessions at which the user handbook can be distributed.

Careful attention to contents and adherence to the handbook preparation procedure should provide the reference material required by user and data center personnel to coordinate their activities and improve the efficiency and reliability of service.

CONCLUSION

This chapter has provided some ground rules for establishing documentation standards. The task remains incomplete, however, until management finds a way to ensure adherence to these standards. To accomplish this, documentation must be an integral part of all system development and modification activities and must be included in the budgets for these activities. With the support of upper management and enforcement of the requirement that no system will go into production without acceptable documentation, the documentation function should assume new importance and receive appropriate attention. Occasionally, of course, systems may be accepted without adequate documentation because of legal requirements or critical deadlines, but this should be permitted only by special approval and with the understanding that the system is accepted on the condition that documentation will be supplied by a stated date.

In addition, a follow-up procedure should be devised for monitoring and evaluating the results of the new documentation standards. If everything is proceeding as planned, activities will progress more smoothly and efficiently, employee morale will improve, and users' faith in obtaining reliable service will increase.

APPENDIX

Sample Procedures

DATA SUBMISSION FOR BATCH PROCESSING

I. Introduction

This procedure applies to DP operations and user personnel. Selected departments (e.g., payroll) require a separate procedure structured to meet special requirements.

The procedure and related forms describe the standard paperwork and processing flow for controlling batches and submission of input by the user to DP, input logging and processing by DP, and the return of source documents to the user. Basic objectives are to:

- Ensure that the flow of input is properly documented
- Validate completion of each processing step required to batch, submit, log, process, and return completed batches
- Provide an effective means of communication among user, data entry, and data control personnel

Any request for deviation from this procedure must be submitted to the DP operations director (or, alternatively, to the manager of data entry operations).

II. Procedure

A. User Department: User personnel will batch and deliver input to MIS operations as follows:

1. Batch input.

a. Input is batched by type of transaction (e.g., stock option), and a batch is not to contain more than one type of transaction.

b. A batch of documents should not be thicker than one inch.

c. Batches must be placed in a folder and bound securely.

d. Each batch must have a "DP input batch control" slip attached. (Refer to Section III for instructions on preparing a batch control slip.)

2. Deliver input batch(es) to data entry.

a. Make certain that the batch control slip is attached to every batch.

b. Deliver batches to data entry input counter as follows:

—Remove the batch control slip(s), and clock it (them) in.

—After clocking, retain a copy of the slip(s) as confirmation of delivery date and time to MIS.

—Attach remaining copies of the slip(s) to the batch(es).

—Place batch(es) on data entry input counter.

B. Data Control: When writing and verification are completed, data entry personnel will submit tape or cards and user input documents to data control.

       1.   Retain the completed batch(es) in data control until proofing or processing is completed.

       2.   When processing has been completed, return input batch(es) to the user department.

III. **Completion Instructions**

    A.   Batch Control Slip

       1.   Divisions

          a. Original (white): data entry

          b. Second copy (yellow): data entry

          c. Third copy (pink): user department

          d. Fourth copy (gold): user department

       2.   Date submitted: date of input submission to MIS data entry

       3.   Group number: the group to which the batch belongs

       4.   User batch number: number assigned by user to control the batches being submitted

       5.   Number of documents submitted: number of documents within a specific batch

UNSCHEDULED JOBS

I. **Introduction**

These procedures and related forms describe the standard paperwork and processing flow for the scheduling, control, and follow-up of all special user requests. Special requests are deviations from the normal processing schedule. They include but are not limited to holiday scheduling, special computer runs, additional copies of an output report (temporary or permanent), searches, and extra sets of labels. Basic objectives are to:

- Ensure that special requests are properly channeled for timely processing
- Provide a record of all such requests for management review and follow-up, if applicable

Any request for deviation from the provisions of this procedure must be submitted to the MIS operations director (or, alternatively, to the manager of scheduling and production control).

II. **Procedure**

    A.   Submit all special requests to the scheduling and production control department (attention: scheduler) in writing. The request must include what is required, when it is required, and who is to be contacted if questions arise.

    B.   If a written request is received by anyone other than the scheduler, that request must be forwarded to the scheduler immediately.

    C.   Within operations, only the scheduler can authorize a special request. The scheduler will communicate with the user. Procedure for the scheduler is as follows:

       1.   Upon receipt of a special request, complete Sections 2, 3, 4,

5, and 6 of the *Special Request Control Log.* Refer to Section III for completion instructions.

2. Based on preassigned tasks or in consultation with the manager of scheduling and production control, determine to whom the request should be assigned.
3. If the scheduled completion time disagrees with the user request, contact the user to determine an alternate date. If no alternative is possible, the matter should be brought to the attention of the manager of scheduling and production control to resolve the difference.
4. Distribute a copy of the special request control log to operations supervision personnel twice each week.

III. Completion Instructions

    A.   Special Request Control Log

1. Fiscal month: a new log will be started each month.
2. Request number: a 4-digit sequential number starting with 0001; each month, the number starts again with 0001.
3. Date submitted: date received by the scheduler.
4. Requested by: name of user department (e.g., payroll).
5. Requested by: name of a manager or supervisor.
6. Request type: identify the type of request (e.g., search, extra set of labels).
7. Date assigned: the date the request is assigned to the individual responsible for its completion.

4 Developing a Data Center Scheduling System

by Daniel A. Pagano
and Richard E. Petrelli

INTRODUCTION

Every manager is familiar with the "things to do list." This list is not unlike the list of jobs that the data center must undertake every day. The data center staff must make decisions about which jobs to process first, second, and so on. Under ideal circumstances a manager can work through his things-to-do list and eventually clear his desk. In reality, however, this seldom happens, and it is sometimes hard to determine why so little is accomplished. A lack of productivity can be caused by unexpected problems, waiting for someone else to complete another job, having something "fall through the cracks," or any of the other situations managers face each day. It would be relatively simple for a manager to plan his time if he were not dependent on other people and outside influences. Similarly, the data center is dependent on the cooperation of its users for the smooth performance of many of its functions. Ensuring that input is submitted on time; checking, keypunching, editing, and updating it; producing reports; saving outputs; and so on are difficult tasks, even on a relatively simple system. When scheduling involves more than a single component or resource, the complexity grows geometrically.

This complexity is obvious if the number of components involved from the time a job enters the data center until it departs are considered. Although the task is difficult, a properly scheduled data center can offer the DCOM an invaluable tool for managing data center resources. Proper scheduling enables the DCOM to plan for and justify personnel, equipment, and facilities needs, without guesswork. There is probably no better tool than a scheduling system to help the DCOM understand his environment. This chapter discusses the reasons for implementing a scheduling system, the various functions that can be scheduled, and the characteristics of manual and automated scheduling systems.

WHO NEEDS A SCHEDULING SYSTEM?

The DCOM who does not have a scheduling system probably suffers from one or more of the problems described in this section. The ever-increasing size of budgets, caused to a great extent by the more specialized use of

equipment and personnel, justifies the need for better control of the environment. Today, many data centers function as service-bureau operations within
their own organizations. They service a broad spectrum of users and extend
computer power to many applications and problem-solving needs. New technology and the distribution and specialization of hardware and personnel have
developed to meet these new demands. In many cases, the user himself has a
terminal directly connected to the computer. All of these factors have increased the complexity of the data center.

Decisions regarding who runs first are much more complex and require
planning more than ever before. The DCOM should consider his particular
situation and check for the symptomatic problems discussed in this chapter.
DCOMs who already have some form of a scheduling system may have some
control over these problems; improving the current system may help to resolve them. DCOMs without scheduling systems may have problems and be
unable to see the underlying causes. This is a difficult situation to correct, and
without a system to help the DCOM ''get a handle'' on what is happening, he
can only attempt to solve the problems through intuition. Implementing a
scheduling system may not solve all problems, but it will at least indicate the
real causes of the problems. The following paragraphs discuss common conditions that are often symptoms of a scheduling problem.

Unhappy Users

The first sign of a major problem is often woeful complaints from users.
Every DCOM confronts this situation at one point or another; to do so without
the aid of meaningful scheduling data makes the job even more difficult. It is
one thing to apologize for a problem and know how to resolve it; it is quite
another if the DCOM does not understand why the problem occurred. The
DCOM may actually be apologizing for a problem caused by the user. To
avoid such situations, the DCOM should be able to effectively track what
happened. Every data center staff makes mistakes. If these errors cannot be
pinpointed, however, they may recur. A good scheduling system enables the
DCOM to compare planned events with actual events and to improve the job
flow.

User Misperception

In many cases when users are unhappy about the quality of service, they
have little data to substantiate their claims. The DCOM is responsible for
considering these complaints, regardless of the lack of supporting data. Often,
long hours can be spent trying to shed some light on the problem. In some
cases, there is really no problem, except in the mind of the user. Although
more computer technology is being placed directly in user hands, many users
still understand little about what goes on in a data center. Often the DCOM
deals with user managers who only know there is a problem because they
constantly hear complaints about the data center.

As a service bureau, the data center is subject to the accuracy and integrity of the staff in the user area. If the DCOM does not maintain his own controls, he cannot tell, for example, that the reason a particular report is always late is the input never arrives on time. The DCOM should be in a position to hold his own staff and, to some extent, his users accountable for their actions. Without the data available from a scheduling system, it is very difficult to solve problems caused by user misperception.

Equipment Underutilization

Equipment underutilization is a difficult problem to solve because factors beyond the control of the scheduling system can contribute to this condition. Scheduling cannot completely overcome the effects of a poorly configured system nor improve poor operator performance; however, an effective scheduling system can help the DCOM to deal more effectively with these problems by enabling him to identify the real cause of the problem through the controls and management feedback provided by a good system.

Equipment Overutilization or Imbalance

Scheduling can help correct work load imbalances within the limits of acceptable user turnaround. Like underutilization, overutilization can be a very deceptive problem. Here again, proper scheduling may not totally resolve the problem, but it will help the DCOM to deal with it more effectively and give management a basis for determining proper solutions. Without proper scheduling, the DCOM can never justify requests for additional equipment.

PRESENTING A CASE TO MANAGEMENT

Once the DCOM is convinced that a scheduling system is needed, he must justify his plans to senior management. This is a very important step; any project of this size should have the endorsement of senior management before it is undertaken. The DCOM should also remember that users will be affected by the implementation of a scheduling system and must themselves commit to cooperation with the data center. Both users and data center personnel should know that the project has the support of senior management. Winning this support may be difficult, particularly if company politics is involved (and most organizations have their favored groups). The DCOM can overcome these problems by justifying the system based on what it will accomplish for the organization as a whole.

Making Management Understand the Problem

The first part of the presentation to senior management, whether written or oral, should not focus on what the DCOM's problems are but on their impact on the organization. Senior management is usually not interested in the details of operations, and they should not be expected to be. Senior management does want to know what the potential benefits of a project are and what resources are necessary to achieve them. The DCOM should be honest about his requirements. If there is currently no scheduling in the data center, the DCOM will need to hire or develop at least one person whose full-time responsibility will be scheduling. An effective scheduling system requires this commitment. Even automated scheduling systems require personnel to make decisions as well as machine resources to produce the schedule and analyze the results.

Getting Support for the Project. As previously stated, senior management is usually interested in the benefits that can be achieved through a project and the resource commitments required. If scheduling is presented as a restrictive control on the availability of data center resources, it will be very difficult to win support. The DCOM should explain to management and users how the scheduling system will make everyone's job easier by adding predictability to the environment and by holding down costs through better utilization of personnel and equipment. Furthermore, there must be benefits outside the data center if the DCOM is to win support for the project. Users will not care how efficiently the data center operates if they continue to receive their output late. The scheduling system will be approved only if both the data center and the users make (and keep) commitments and if there are measurable benefits for both areas.

Benefits of the System. The most important part of scheduling, and the true measure of how well the DCOM understands his environment, is the set of goals the DCOM establishes for the scheduling system. If the DCOM does not clearly understand the benefits he expects from the system, it will be impossible to achieve them; you cannot hit a target you cannot see. It is very important to understand the performance objectives clearly and present them effectively to management and users.

POLICY IMPLICATIONS OF SCHEDULING

Data center scheduling requires commitments from user departments or clients in order to observe firm deadlines for submission of input and to allow the DP department enough time to deliver a quality product. If scheduling is to be effective, the organization must have a written policy or management directive listing the relative importance of the applications being processed. Such a priority list enables the DCOM to develop scheduling policies consistent with organizational objectives.

Scheduling in a DP organization usually results from a need for improved efficiency. Data centers sometimes find it difficult to establish or meet user deadlines because of hardware and/or software constraints. In such cases the DCOM should call upon management for policy decisions, particularly when the resolution of scheduling conflicts involves hardware/software acquisition rather than rescheduling. Most scheduling problems can be resolved by acquiring additional or larger hardware or by converting to more efficient systems software. As many DCOMs have learned over the years, however, hardware/software acquisition is not always the answer. In fact, the DCOM who acquires equipment without first determining whether user requirements can be met on existing equipment through improved scheduling is squandering financial resources.

Senior management cannot be involved in the resolution of day-to-day computer service problems. The data center ultimately has responsibility for servicing all user departments, and management policy guidelines should give the DCOM responsibility for resolving any scheduling conflicts. These guidelines should be made available to all users.

User and Data Center Commitment

Today's users are gaining more and more knowledge about the potential uses of computers in their environments. As a result, requests for data center services become more backlogged. By this point, data center clients should understand the relationship of input to output. Users are certainly aware that if the input provided is "garbage," the output will be similarly poor; however, many users do not appreciate the amount of time and effort necessary for the data center to process their jobs correctly. Management, users, and data center personnel must all realize that the data center must have a reasonable period of time to process the work.

Most users do not understand that much more than computer time is necessary to produce quality output. This is an education problem. The preprocessing and postprocessing steps associated with a given application system may involve many manual and/or automated procedures requiring hours, while the computer may only require minutes, to process the job. Even the most generous studies have shown that no more than 10 percent of a job's lifetime is spent in the computer.

Users should be educated on the DP state of the art and should understand the points discussed in the following sections.

Batch Applications. These applications usually require little actual computer time compared with the time spent in the manual efforts needed to produce the finished product.

Online Data Entry and Edit Applications. Users of these applications should understand that although they are interacting directly with the computer system, they are simply generating a clean transaction for later updating through batch programs. Online data collection eliminates such manual steps as data transcription, data keying, data verification, and automated edit runs; however, users should realize that inquiries will not reflect the most recently input transactions. Users in this environment often fail to understand the batc' work required after the terminal network is brought down.

Online Data Base Update Applications. Users of these appl' should understand the complexities involved in handling a computer with many online terminals, as well as the potential time delays that result when the system services many transactions concurrently.

While eliminating many preprocessing steps, online systems make the scheduling problem more complex, affecting the data center in the following three ways:

- Consuming a significant portion of machine resources during prime-shift hours
- Reducing the time available for batch activity against online files, since most data centers try to avoid processing batch jobs that may degrade terminal response
- Adding a significant batch work load to the data center in the areas of file recovery, backup, and reorganization

Work Flow Analysis

Regardless of the types of systems in a particular environment, every organization has a formal or informal work load structure that encompasses all of the functional areas in the data center. Figure 4-1 illustrates a typical data center work flow structure for a batch-only environment. As pointed out previously, the presence of online systems (unless highly sophisticated) only eliminates the data entry and data control functions. Moreover, online systems complicate the overall scheduling process. The DCOM who understands the work flow in his data center and helps the user understand its complexity will be in a better position to negotiate reasonable user schedules.

The DCOM should prepare a formal presentation to the user community, using graphic materials such as the chart shown in Figure 4-1. Before giving this presentation, the DCOM should collect data on jobs that are pertinent to the users to whom the presentation will be made. If the users understand the time constraints under which the data center functions, it will be easier for the DCOM to obtain user adherence to schedules. On the other hand, the DCOM must understand the requirements for processing a given user's work and be prepared to make similar commitments.

Identifying Critical Areas in the Data Center

In the production-oriented environment found in most medium- to large-scale data centers, the DCOM deals with multiple user deadlines, applications, source-document inputs, application and utility programs, tape files, disk files, card files, output reports, and so on. In addition, the DCOM must be concerned with the quality and quantity of the work performed in the center and the effective utilization of staff, inventory consumables, computer time, and tape and disk libraries. For these reasons, DCOMs in data centers of this type should schedule at least the more critical resources. The most critical resource is usually the computer itself because it has always been the single most costly item in the data center; however, taking into consideration the increases in personnel costs and the decreases in hardware costs in recent years, it is more appropriate to examine the total operation of the data center.

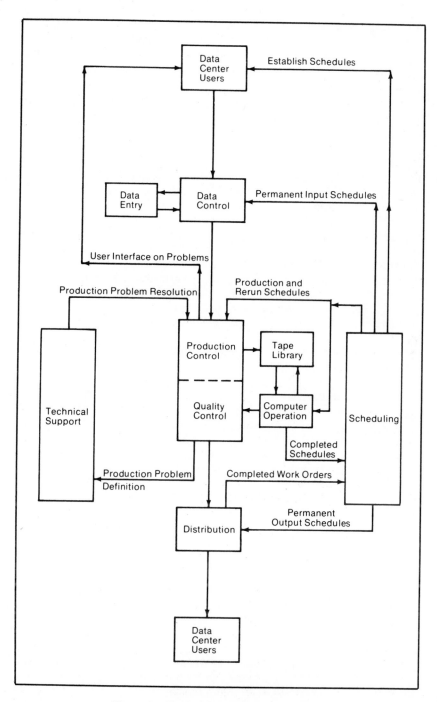

Figure 4-1. Typical Data Center Work Flow

Mapping Data Center Functions

Beginning with the work-flow diagram in Figure 4-1 and an organization chart, the DCOM should identify each function essential to the production process. Associated functions should be classified into workstations.

A typical operations organization is composed of four working sections:
- Computer Operations
- Technical Support
- Scheduling
- I/O Control

Each has specific functional responsibilities for segments of the work flow (see Figure 4-1). These functional responsibilities can be outlined by section, as is indicated in the following paragraphs

Computer Operations. The primary responsibility of computer operations is to operate the computer and associated peripherals in accordance with authorized schedules. This group must also:
- Receive jobs and associated processing instructions from production control or scheduling
- Update schedules as the work is completed
- Forward all output to the quality-control section

Technical Support. The primary responsibility of this group is to provide technical support for production systems and to resolve problems. This group must also:
- Determine the source of errors and take corrective action
- Initiate problem reports as required and insure that problems are resolved in a timely manner.

Scheduling. The primary responsibility of the scheduling section is to make production commitments for the data center and provide processing schedules for input, output, production control, and computer operations. Scheduling should also coordinate the activities of the tape library.

I/O Control. This section performs several functions within a data center:
- Data Control—The primary responsibility of this group is to receive input from users and coordinate the input work flow through the data center. This group must also:
  —Count and verify documents received from users by total documents received, hash totals, and control tapes
  —Edit all source documents for legibility, and verify dates and user departments
  —Verify that the input volume correlates with anticipated schedules
  —Log all data by sequence number
  —Forward data to the correct workstation, as indicated in procedures
  —Cross-reference input data and schedules
  —Coordinate the receipt of late data with users and the data center

- Production Control—The primary responsibility of this group is to prepare jobs for computer processing. This group also acts as a liaison between the data center and the user community and must also:
  —Initiate processing orders for all production jobstreams
  —Accept input from the data control group
  —Process work in accordance with procedures
  —Notify the tape librarian of input tape requirements
  —Update processing orders
  —Submit jobs to operations
  —Contact users in special situations only
  —Store and maintain completed JCL listings
- Quality Control—The primary responsibility of this group is to review all output from computer operations and determine its correctness and completeness before it is forwarded to distribution. This group must also:
  —Receive all output from computer operations
  —Verify all production output
  —Forward output to technical support if outputs are incomplete or incorrect
  —Forward JCL to scheduling
  —Forward tests to programmers
- Distribution—The primary responsibility of this group is to distribute all outputs in a timely fashion. Distribution will maintain control logs on completed reports and ensure the proper delivery of reports to the users. This group must also:
  —Receive output from the quality-control group
  —Process and package reports, and forward them to users
  —Collect receipts for all accepted output
- Data Entry—The primary responsibility of this group is to convert source documents into computer-acceptable form using a key-entry machine. This group must also:
  —Accept source documents
  —Key-enter and verify all inputs
  —Maintain work load controls, and report accordingly
  —Review output quality
  —Return completed batch data to the data control clerk

By mapping all data center functions and defining their interrelationships, the DCOM can generate a work flow diagram for his particular environment. In an organization such as the one depicted in the preceding paragraphs, there are only two workstations that are not candidates for scheduling: technical support (because of its problem orientation) and scheduling itself.

Deciding Which Functions Need Scheduling

Unless the DCOM decides to schedule all data center functions and is prepared to make a commitment for the necessary personnel, money, and (perhaps) machine resources, he must decide which functions should be scheduled. If this is the DCOM's first attempt at scheduling, it might be prudent to single out one or two functions to schedule. On such a first attempt, the DCOM wants the impact of the scheduling system to be highly visible and measurable; therefore, he should identify those areas where bottlenecks affect the most critical work. Scheduling these areas will achieve maximum impact. The DCOM should not make the mistake of scheduling a function offering less visible results simply because it appears that this particular function would be easier to schedule.

Scheduling Noncomputer Resources

Proper scheduling can improve the utilization of any critical resource, whether it is a machine, a project, or a person. Proper scheduling of critical resources can also make possible a previously unattainable flexibility in completing production requirements.

There may be reasons for scheduling departmental resources other than the computer itself. In DP organizations, this usually means scheduling human resources. It is relatively simple to schedule human resources once an accurate profile of the data center work flow has been established. This profile will enable the scheduler to predict turnaround times based on past experience. The most important element in scheduling all human resources is to provide start and stop times and sufficient time to perform the function while maintaining an even work flow. The functions listed in the following paragraphs are the noncomputer resources that are most often scheduled.

Input Control. It is almost essential to schedule this function since the input control group is required to track all inputs. Late input almost always necessitates alteration of the schedule; also, some form of notification should be sent to the user. Each input coming into the data center should be edited. The input clerk should know not only when the input is to arrive but when it is due in data entry, the next function to be performed.

Data Entry. Data entry usually involves both initial key entry and key verification. The data entry section should be aware of the time the input is due from the users, the approximate number of documents expected, and the time the input is due for processing. Within this period, there should be sufficient time for the data entry function to be performed.

Data Control. The data control section frequently reports directly to the scheduler in order to keep data control aware of all scheduling concerns and vice versa. The scheduler should inform data control of the time the job is due on and off the computer and the time the job should be forwarded for distribution. Sufficient time should be provided for job setup, JCL preparation, and a complete check of all outputs. Reruns and late arrivals should be brought to the scheduler's attention immediately in order to keep the entire department operating smoothly.

Output Control. This function can be scheduled by providing those responsible for output with the time the output is due for distribution and the time it is due to the user. This allows output control to determine the most cost-effective method for distributing subject reports. This type of scheduling is particularly useful if the reports are shipped or mailed to distant locations.

User Input Schedules. The unavailability of machine-readable input data may cause delays in scheduling the computer or completing output. Because of these consequences, the DCOM should consider scheduling users, particularly if he can determine that the cause for delay in meeting user deadlines is in the user area rather than in the DP department. In a remote job entry (RJE) environment, it is very important to schedule user input, since all jobs submitted are eligible for immediate processing.

User Output Schedules. Few, if any, data centers have the luxury of setting their own schedules for output reports to users. Far too many data centers allow users or systems analysts to dictate requirements regarding dates and times that reports are due in a user department. Scheduling user output is a necessity, requiring data center involvement before the systems are accepted for production. When this is done, unachievable demands can be identified quickly. If the data center is not involved in these decisions, the demands may be accepted by someone in the DP department, and operations must then fight the too-familiar battles to get the schedules changed. Even worse, the analysts may ignore the time needed to produce the desired outputs and may not realize that a different solution (e.g., an online system) is actually needed. If a data center is to provide effective results, it must have some control over the schedule for distributing reports to users.

Scheduling the Computer

Although any critical resource can be scheduled to achieve more flexibility in operations, the one resource scheduled in most data centers is the computer itself. Block scheduling, the simplest form of scheduling, dedicates all or a portion of a particular resource to a given function during certain hours of the day. This type of scheduling is generally used to resolve relatively simple problems. However simple in concept, block scheduling is the basis for all types of scheduling. Applying this simple technique to the computer is made more difficult by:
- The capability of a third-generation-plus machine to process several jobs concurrently
- The interdependence of jobs in such an environment
- The dependence of jobs on I/O devices and/or particular data sets
- The number of each type of device available to the system at a given time
- The availability of memory
- The availability of machine-readable input data

Given the items just listed, the scheduling system must track, overlay, integrate, and interrelate block schedules for each of the available operating system and hardware components.

MANUAL VERSUS AUTOMATED SCHEDULING

One of the key decisions to be made when developing a scheduling system is whether to use a manual or automated system. Much more must be considered than the cost of a package to automate the scheduling function versus the current investment in talent in the data center. This section deals with the issues that should be considered in making this decision and includes a comparison of the two approaches. This is a very critical decision because the investment for the system will be significant and a wrong decision can be costly. A manual system may seem like the safest choice since it can be converted into an automated system; however, this is not always the case. The standards developed for a manual system may have to be changed, and people will have to be retrained for such a conversion. These changes can result in significant costs.

Characteristics of a Manual System

Manual scheduling systems can and do work well. Many data centers have used manual methods successfully for years. There are advantages and disadvantages to this approach, each of which should be weighed as it relates to the DCOM's organization. A manual system can bring the following advantages:

- Simple block scheduling techniques—Manual systems are characterized by the use of simple block scheduling methods. The advantage of this methodology is that it is easily understood by management, users, and data center personnel, thereby enabling easy implementation of the schedule for all concerned.
- Machine-independent—Manual schedules are usually developed at a desk. There is little, if any, need for the use of the computer to produce the schedule.
- Less up-front cost—Manual systems usually have a low start-up cost because primary materials for the system are forms and scheduling boards. These items are inexpensive compared with the price of an automated scheduling package.
- More personal—Because the manual system uses simple scheduling techniques, it is more easily understood by the personnel it affects. A personal touch, which is lost in the technical details of an automated system, is possible with a manual system. In some data centers, the personal handling of problems between users and the scheduling department helps to maintain a high level of DP credibility.
- Short development time—Because manual systems require no programming and use a forms approach, they can usually be developed in a relatively short period of time. This can be helpful if current scheduling problems are severe and a quick solution is required.
- Allows evolution to an automated system—If a manual system is prop-

erly designed and installed, the standards employed should allow the system to be automated if required. This consideration is important in a small data center that is growing rapidly. On the other hand, it may be very difficult to change from an automated system to a manual system without embarrassment to the DCOM and considerable inconvenience to the organization.

- Small-organization use—A manual system can be the best approach for the small data center or the center with a low work load level. Many of the advantages of the automated approach are negated if the data center has excess capacity; in such cases a manual approach may more than suffice.

The disadvantages of a manual scheduling system should also be considered:

- People dependent—A manual scheduling system requires personnel to develop and maintain the operating schedules. Before choosing a manual system the DCOM should seriously consider the capability of his staff in order to ensure that the talent and time needed to make the system effective are available.
- Problems projecting the impact of changes—Manual systems cannot instantly reschedule everything in response to an operating or user crisis. Because of this, it is difficult to predict the future impact of priority changes, especially if many functions are scheduled. This is a fundamental weakness in manual systems, although a good scheduler who really knows the shop can do a fairly good job making such changes. In a large center, however, it is almost impossible to perform this task manually. The DCOM should consider whether the frequency of rescheduling in his data center warrants the installation of an automated system.
- Fewer considerations can be handled—Because of limitations, manual systems typically deal with fewer scheduling considerations than do automated systems. It is usually difficult to consider factors beyond date/time due and predecessor-successor relationships. Some of these factors can be important, particularly if the schedule is tight because they can improve throughput by making scheduling more effective. These factors include CPU to I/O mix in the system, increasing run-time experience with a job during a processing cycle, and so on.
- Less accuracy and more susceptibility to judgment errors—Because manual systems typically use less data to develop the schedule and because of unavoidable human errors, manual systems are less accurate than automated systems. This may not be crucial if the center has effective backup/restore procedures. If a data center is overloaded and a significant percentage of the work is reruns, a manual system may not reduce reruns as much as desired. In addition, since scheduling personnel usually deal with production jobs, they often have difficulty making proper decisions about priorities for test work.
- Difficulty plotting history or predicting trends—Most manual systems are designed to schedule the current activities of the data center rather

than to track past activities. The absence of this capability makes it difficult to use the system to analyze historical developments or to project trends. This may be a serious shortcoming in a rapidly expanding environment where good planning data is a must.

- Tendency to overkill—Some data centers always run the most critical job in the shop first, regardless of when the job is due; their only scheduling criteria are the availability of the job and its criticality. This is a nonproductive method of scheduling because it pays little attention to noncritical jobs and programmer testing. Often programmers are left idle while the data center runs jobs that could be scheduled at night. This is a very wasteful practice, and manual systems can do little to restrict it.

Characteristics of Automated Systems

Automated scheduling systems vary widely in capability and cost. This includes systems developed in-house. Most automated systems offer the following advantages:

- Standards enforcement—For an organization that has standards or wants to implement them, one of the advantages of an automated system is that it can enforce such standards as job numbers, job names, program numbers, account numbers, and so on.
- Trend analysis—An effective automated system provides the ability to examine data center trends. Trends can be predicted for a single job, an application, or the whole system and can be helpful for projecting future work loads on a given system.
- Disaster and capacity planning—Many automated systems allow the data center to identify disaster backup requirements by automatically identifying file updates. An automated system can also be useful as a modeling tool in capacity planning. By running a proposed configuration on the scheduling system, planners can predict the benefits of adding, upgrading, or reducing equipment.
- Priorities and unforeseen work load handling—Although it may require a scheduling run through the computer, a good automated system can show the impact of changing priorities or adding new work. In such situations the DCOM may only be able to get the "hot job" out, but at least he can notify other users of delays before they actually occur. This is helpful if delays are significant. An automated system also works to minimize the impact of the change by attempting to catch up as quickly as possible. It is conceivable that a priority change could necessitate a complete rescheduling, and an automated system can accomplish this much faster than a manual system.
- Throughput optimization within scheduling constraints—A good scheduling system will optimize throughput if the input is available early enough to allow flexibility.
- Self-educating—A good system can "educate" itself as it gains experience with a particular job, enabling it to schedule the work into tighter

time frames and to be more precise about the requirements for running the job.

- Better production/nonproduction work load mix—automated systems schedule based on time due out and resources required. If production work is entered into the system early enough, the scheduler should attempt to optimize throughput by mixing work that runs well together. It is also possible to reserve periods of time for programmer testing by having the scheduler give priority to testing unless a production commitment is due.
- High accuracy—Under normal circumstances, automated systems will never forget to schedule a job. Automated systems are accurate even in long-range scheduling. This is useful when planning new applications or jobs because it enables planners to determine the impact of the new addition over a longer period of time.
- Adaptable to growth—Because of their ability to track the history of jobs and examine trends, automated systems are very adaptable in situations where the data center is growing quickly. In such an environment the scheduling system may be the only reliable source of planning data.
- People independent—Automated systems allow the scheduling group to code scheduling logic without programming. Once coded, these systems are not dependent on personnel. A good system should be well documented and easy to learn, further reducing dependence on particular individuals in the organization.
- High start-up costs—Whether developed internally or purchased, most automated systems will have a high start-up cost. In an organization with limited resources, this can be a serious shortcoming. The DCOM must ensure that sufficient resources exist to implement the system. If there are any doubts, the DCOM may want to consider lower-cost options or a manual system.
- Long development time—Because of the sophistication of the data used for scheduling and the length of time needed to develop or tailor programs, an automated scheduling system usually has a long development time. If the DCOM wants immediate benefits, he should consider another approach, at least on an interim basis.
- Standardization—If the DCOM's organization has no standards (particularly for job numbering), he will have difficulty implementing an automated system. Standards have benefits in themselves and should be considered by all organizations; however, if they do not exist and will not be developed, the DCOM should consider another scheduling approach.

Comparison of Manual and Automated Systems

The DCOM should carefully consider the degree to which the characteristics discussed previously will positively or negatively affect his data center. The following paragraphs provide additional information on the two types of systems.

Accuracy. Although manual systems can be very accurate, the degree of accuracy depends on the quality of the personnel involved, the usability of the system, and the number of items to be considered. Automated systems are very accurate and self-educating, both in recognizing new jobs entered into the system and in keeping track of job durations.

Costs. Manual systems are usually less expensive to develop, install, and maintain. Because they are personnel dependent, however, there is a point at which these systems can become fairly expensive to operate. Although they have a high start-up cost, automated systems are generally inexpensive to maintain, especially if purchased from an outside vendor.

Flexibility. Although seemingly flexible, manual systems cannot easily handle unforeseen work loads and problem situations without seriously affecting an already-planned schedule. In most manual systems, scheduling changes cause as many problems as they resolve; however, this can be prevented if changes are controlled by knowledgeable scheduling personnel. Automated systems facilitate schedule changes while attempting to optimize the schedule within available constraints.

Efficiency Measurement. In manual systems, measurements of scheduled versus actual efficiency are rarely made. The purpose of such measurements is to determine which scheduled jobs did not get done so that they can be rescheduled. With a manual system, the work is rescheduled and ultimately completed; however, scheduling personnel are not apprised of the reasons the original schedule was not followed. An automated system automatically reschedules incompleted work, measures itself, and takes corrective action to improve future schedules.

Billing. In manual systems it is possible, but rare, to link scheduling functions to computer billing. In automated systems the scheduling data can be fed to an automated billing system for such billing items as reruns, canceled jobs, time slots scheduled, and so on.

Change. Scheduling in a changing environment is facilitated by an automated scheduler with the ability to educate itself and adapt to changes. In a manual system, data center personnel must be reoriented before scheduling changes take effect. An automated system acts as a training tool helping to reorient data center staff during a period of change.

CONCLUSION

A scheduling system can be a valuable tool to aid the DCOM in managing data center resources, improving service to users, and planning for work-load changes. Taking into account the specific characteristics of his environment, the DCOM should determine which functions and resources should be scheduled and decide whether his organization would be better served by a manual or automated scheduling system.

5 Data Center Planning Checklist

by Philip C. Cross

INTRODUCTION

Some degree of formal planning is necessary for every data center. Even if the DCOM does not have to anticipate and accommodate new technology, applications, or work loads, planning is needed to maintain (or improve) service levels and operating efficiencies. Thus, the DCOM must determine what the future holds for the data center and must also set priorities properly to satisfy changing demands while maximizing cost/service trade-offs.

Even when every effort is made to plan as accurately and as realistically as possible, it is highly unlikely that actual performance will match the plan. The complexities of data center operation and changing user pressures always cause actual conditions to vary from those originally anticipated. Because of this, it is necessary to provide means for:

- Measuring planned against actual performance
- Changing the plan when it appears that events will not occur as expected

Continually measuring performance against planned objectives ensures that plans are kept current and pertinent and also affords data center management a means for measuring its own performance.

Although this planning process may appear straightforward, it is far from simple. It is full of pitfalls for the DCOM who lacks a disciplined approach to planning.

This chapter presents a series of questions that the DCOM should ask to understand how to develop a realistic data center plan.

GOALS AND OBJECTIVES

Does a Formalized Methodology Exist for Setting Goals and Objectives as a Basis for Planning? The distinction between goals and objectives is often debated. The most widely accepted view, however, is a hierarchical relationship in which:

- Goals explain a desirable status
- Objectives define the behavior or performance required to attain that status

Some examples applicable to data center planning include:

- Goal—Provide high service levels.
  Objective—Average less than a five-second response time per type A transaction.
- Goal—Support development teams.
  Objective—Average less than a two-hour test printout turnaround.
- Goal—Improve user interface.
  Objective—Conduct user meetings once every three months.

Of course, meeting one goal may require that more than one objective be satisfied. Providing high service levels, for example, may involve objectives in many areas in addition to online response time. Using goals and objectives in this manner provides a structured and logical approach for data center planning.

Have User Departments Defined Goals and Objectives That the Data Center Can Support? If the user departments' goals and objectives are unclear, the DCOM should request that they be accurately defined. If this effort is unsuccessful, the DCOM must avoid setting data center goals and objectives that:

- Place the interests or preferences of the data center above user needs
- Simply maintain the status quo

A lack of clearly defined user goals creates a difficult situation for the DCOM and makes it much more difficult to ensure that the data center meets the organization's needs. The DCOM should therefore do his or her best to ensure that user departments identify DP-related goals and objectives.

Do User Goals and Objectives Explain What Is Needed to Achieve Them? Very general user goals and objectives can actually obscure critical needs. For example, deadlines for the development of a new or enhanced application cannot be met if the computer time allotted for testing and development is inadequate. It is therefore in the best interests of both the DCOM and the users to stipulate as precisely as possible what the users expect from the data center.

Does Senior Management Understand and Approve Data Center Goals and Objectives and Provide the Resources Needed to Achieve Them? Senior management often does not fully appreciate the extent to which achieving goals and objectives depends on the availability of data center resources (i.e., funding, personnel, and facilities). If the DCOM does not ensure that approval for needed critical resources will be granted, it will be difficult to achieve the goals and objectives.

Has the Data Center Avoided Functional Overlap with Other Departments in Setting Goals and Objectives? Functional overlap can occur when a department focuses too intently on performing functional tasks. It is impossible to completely eliminate overlapping within an organization or even within a department such as the data center. Sometimes overlap is deliberately induced to provide checks and balances. Clearly defined goals and objectives can help identify undesirable overlaps that, even if not always eliminated, can at least be brought to the surface, thereby avoiding polarization or conflict among departments.

If the organization has an official planning department, or if someone in the organization has been designated to oversee planning, this department or person can review the data center's goals and objectives to ensure that they fit into the "big picture."

Do Data Center Goals and Objectives Take into Account the Effect of Administrative Support or Service Departments? The DCOM would be foolish to commit to goals and objectives without knowing for certain that the support services needed from other departments will be forthcoming. Such services include:

- Administrative support
  —Typing, copying, printing
  —Contract review and content approval
  —Purchasing and vendor awards
- User department support
  —Work load forecasting
  —Application operating documentation
  —Conformance to standards

Unfortunately, the DCOM often takes such support for granted, even with new or expanded services, only to find later that it will not be provided.

Do All Data Center Managers Understand Their Individual Contributions to the Goals and Objectives? Unless each manager understands precisely how data center goals and objectives relate to his or her responsibilities, the coordinated effort needed to achieve those goals and objectives can be hampered.

Once each manager knows what is expected from his or her area, the next step is to involve the managers in the planning process in order to make the plan as realistic as possible and to have them identify and agree to their specific responsibilities.

Are Data Center Goals and Objectives Viewed from the Double Perspective of Project Support and Operational Performance? The DCOM should see goals and objectives from two standpoints:

- Project support—These goals and objectives focus on efforts that support user-department projects (either through direct participation or through provision of facilities, technology, or an operating environment that best aids user departments in new application development, application installation, and online transaction tuning).
- Operational performance—These goals and objectives deal with efficient and effective operation of the data center. They focus on such efforts as:

—Reducing expenses
—Maintaining high morale
—Improving user communications

Do Operational Goals Focus on Performance Improvements? Goals and objectives for such areas as service levels (e.g., turnaround, problem solving, response times, disk storage, CPU utilization) and expense performance (e.g., chargeback, supplies, maintenance, hardware acquisition) should address the following questions:

- What is current performance?
- What should performance be?
- What actions are needed to reach desired levels?
- How long will it take to reach these levels?

The answers to these questions offer the DCOM the perspective needed to identify and plan performance improvements.

Do Goals Provide Means to Track Progress and Make Corrections When Needed? Goal setting should include the identification of checkpoints for comparing actual versus planned status. Such checkpoints are built-in reporting mechanisms that signal when deviations or undesirable trends are developing. Checkpoints must accurately measure the appropriate factors to prevent misunderstanding or purposeful distortion.

Are Goals and Objectives Viewed as Opportunities? Viewing goals and objectives as challenges or opportunities can help increase morale. If goals and objectives are too difficult, they may be interpreted as exploitation of the data center. The DCOM should promote an attitude among all data center personnel that regards goals and objectives as opportunities for employees to show how competent they really are.

Are the Goals and Objectives Flexible Enough to Enable Modification If Necessary? Goals and objectives should not be inflexible. During the planning process, the DCOM may find that original goals and objectives are unachievable or that they can be surpassed. Overambitious goals may result from impractical time schedules, inadequate personnel skills, or excessive costs. Such goals should be adjusted to conform with reality. At the other extreme, goals and objectives may be too conservative; in this case, greater progress may be possible.

REQUIREMENTS FORECASTING

Is Requirements Forecasting Considered a Necessary Activity by Both User and Data Center Management? Requirements forecasting is the cornerstone of the planning process. Forecasts must be as complete and as accurate as possible.

Forecasting must be systematized and integrated into the operating and management policies and procedures of the data center; all personnel should be aware that the DCOM considers such forecasts an important aspect of data center management. If forecasting is not taken seriously, data center management will tend to be reactive, and the performance of the data center will depend on how well personnel can cope with problems rather than on how well they can anticipate and avoid them.

Are Users Required to Participate in Forecasting Their Computer Requirements? The DCOM who forecasts requirements without user participation and approval may encounter problems if those forecasts are wrong—particularly when the result is poor service or higher-than-expected user costs.

Is Each User Group Required to Appoint a Forecaster? This arrangement is mandatory if the DCOM is to hold users responsible in the forecasting process. The DCOM should do everything possible to aid the users by providing forms and data to simplify forecasts and making them as accurate and understandable as possible.

Do Users Understand the Extent of the Services Offered? Frequently data center management makes too many assumptions about user department understanding of data center services. Consequently, users make invalid forecasts based on inaccurate information.

Simply because data center service definitions and criteria are explained in operating procedures and user guides does not mean that they are understood by user management. The DCOM should make an extra effort to apprise management of data center services via periodic communiqués.

Do Forecasts Identify Expected Service Levels as well as Volumes? The DCOM should avoid focusing solely on the quantitative (processing-volume) aspect of requirements forecasting, thereby neglecting the qualitative (service-level) aspect. In some cases, a slight increase in service-level quality, which may require increased resources or management attention, has a greater impact on data center operation than does a great increase in volume, which tends to take advantage of economy of scale. The DCOM must, therefore, require that forecasts define expected service levels as well as processing volumes.

Do Forecasts Address Testing and Development Needs as well as Production? Some DCOMs give all production processing a higher priority than testing and development. Generally this is correct, but there may be times when testing and development should take precedence over some types of production processing. In particular, the DCOM who foresees a capacity shortage and does not expect an equipment upgrade must obtain agreement from users and DP senior management on priorities for testing and development, on a project-by-project basis.

The DCOM who provides processing for testing and development on a "catch as catch can" basis often ends up running applications that are poorly tested and implemented. These applications are often unreliable and lack proper operating documentation.

Do Resource Forecasts Clearly Differentiate between Production Processing and System Overhead? As computer applications and capabilities have become more sophisticated and extensive, system overhead has correspondingly risen. This is difficult for user managers to understand. They cannot comprehend, for example, how a computer operating at 90 percent utilization can be only 75 percent productive. Of course, the key to this problem lies in the definitions of utilization and productive. Such terms must be clearly defined for management and should be precisely used in the forecasting process to avoid later misunderstanding or misinterpretation.

Have Peripheral Usage Levels Been Fully Analyzed for New and Expanded Applications? Because DP management tends to center on processors rather than on peripheral equipment, it is easy to neglect or superficially guess at requirements for disk, tape, printing, and telecommunications equipment. Such estimates can be very inaccurate if they are based on experience that is not applicable to new and more sophisticated applications (e.g., data bases, security, telecommunications). Consequently, the DCOM often finds that the utilization for such equipment exceeds planned equipment capabilities.

Do Forecasts Allow for Peak Requirements? Few DCOMs can afford the luxury of spreading work load as they choose so as to balance peaks and valleys and maintain resource usage at the lowest possible level. Instead, they must cope with periods of high and low demand. For example, heavy online activity during the day can saturate disk and telecommunications controllers that stand practically idle at night or on weekends. Tape drives, however, may pose severe bottlenecks at night but may be poorly utilized during the day.

The DCOM must accurately forecast peak demands and determine resource requirements in accordance with these demands and give DP senior management and users valid estimates of the costs involved. Users and management can then determine beforehand if the costs are justified. On the other hand, if peak demands are not forecast, resulting in inadequate services, the blame will rest with the DCOM.

Are Performance Indicators Used to Check the Validity of Forecasts? Where should we be? Where are we? Where should we be going? These questions form the stimulus for effective forecasting. They cannot be answered, however, unless there is some basis for measurement and comparison. That basis is provided by such performance indicators as availability, utilization (by device type), throughput, response time, problem determination and solution, expenditures, and user complaints. If forecasts specifically list how indicators such as these must be satisfied, and if each indicator is measured at specified points, the forecast can be evaluated. These evaluations can then be used as the basis for future forecasting.

Are Forecasts Compared with Past Experience Wherever Feasible? The DCOM should take advantage of hindsight as much as possible to maintain a pragmatic approach to planning. If data center management is inexperienced with new processing methods, an outside consultant can help identify potential forecasting problems and pitfalls.

Are Resource Utilization Forecasts Directly Related to Costs and Revenues? This is important if the data center charges users for services. Forecasts are made to plan for resources that will satisfy user needs as well as for budgeting purposes. It is therefore important for the DCOM to anticipate or at least be able to explain any variances from the budget that result from anticipated demands not being met or any variances that exceed expectations. The forecasts must enable understanding of the financial implications of deviations.

If the Data Center Uses More Than One Type of Computer, Is a Standard Used to Project Computer Requirements? It can be confusing for both technical and administrative personnel to project computer utilization requirements unless a common unit of measure is agreed upon. For example, if two computers are involved and if one of them is half as fast as the other, the standard can indicate that the larger computer is equivalent to two of the smaller computers.

Is the Tuning/Capacity Cost Trade-off Considered When Forecasting Resource Requirements? Fine tuning CPU memory, channels, and disk storage, for example, can reduce the amount of those resources needed. Such tuning, however, may require expensive technicians, sophisticated diagnostic software and hardware, continual manipulation of job classes and priority schemes, and so on until it may be less costly to simply provide additional computing resources. This trade-off should be analyzed when forecasting.

Does the DCOM Require User Management to Approve Forecasts before They Are Formalized? User participation in the forecasting process does not necessarily mean user commitment and accountability. Before the forecasts are formalized and made part of the DP budget, the DCOM should obtain formal commitment from the responsible user managers.

Has a Capacity Model Been Established as a Basis for Projecting Work Load Requirements? A capacity or utilization model depicting current usage must be established as a reference point for forecasters and planners. This model can be used to build on and to refer to if forecasts change.

After Forecasts Are Made, Are Users Informed That Changes in Forecasted Requirements May Lead to Inadequate Service? The DCOM must clarify to users that once resource requirements have been determined (and, in particular, once expense budgets have been established), the data center cannot be expected to satisfy needs that exceed these planned levels.

Are Resources Ordered Far Enough in Advance to Allow Delivery to Be Expedited or Postponed without Penalty? Projecting resource needs and ensuring that the resources will be installed when necessary can be very difficult. User needs can change, application development schedules can slip, and unexpected volume can require installation of a new CPU earlier than expected. It is therefore important that arrangements with vendors allow some leeway—particularly when the resources involved have long delivery intervals and/or are scarce high-demand items that the vendor can easily assign to another customer.

Can Resource Costs Be Linked to the Users Who Have Forecast a Need for Those Resources? Users should be held accountable for their utilization of resources, and additional costs to supplement or support those resources should be charged back or at least attributed to specific users. Frequently the DP buck stops in the data center, not in the user department. This situation can easily lead to inflated DP budgets, insufficient cost control, and users who are far from cost-conscious. Such undesirable conditions can be avoided if the DCOM can show when poor cost performance is a result of poor user performance.

Is the Forecasting Process Linked to the Budgeting Process to Ensure that Hardware, Software, and Telecommunications Acquisitions Are Identified and Expensed on a Monthly Schedule? Any expensed acquisition should be keyed to the budget under the appropriate account category on a cost-and-time basis. This should be done to convince management that such acquisitions have been thoroughly justified and to compare actual progress against forecast—from both financial and project performance standpoints.

⑥ The Data Center Budget: An Overview
by Jagdish R. Dalal

INTRODUCTION

In most instances, the data center is established as a cost center supported directly or indirectly from the profits of the organization. Budget management, therefore, is one of the prime responsibilities of the data center manager. This chapter discusses generally accepted practices for planning, developing, and managing the data center budget. Many of the concepts discussed here can be used in any data center; however, their application may vary depending on the fiscal management policies of the corporation. Because this chapter focuses on the data center budget, the income (or cost distribution) of the center is not discussed.

DEFINITIONS

This review of the data center budget is based on the following definitions and assumptions:
- The data center is an independent entity in the organization and services only the computing needs of the organization.
- The data center has budgetary accountability. For our discussion, it is immaterial whether it is established as a budget center or as a profit center or whether the data center is run on a cost basis, a full charge-back basis, or an overhead basis. These methods of charging for computing services will, for the most part, affect only the development and presentation of budget data and will have little impact on the budgeting process presented here.
- The corporation's accounting system provides the data necessary to manage the data center budget.
- Corporate management includes data center management in the planning and control processes, rather than merely handing the budget to the data center.

The budget is a management tool used for financial planning and control. Depending on the nature of the organization, detailed budgets may be formulated for the next few months, the next year, the next five years, or longer. Different organizations have different nomenclatures and procedures for budget development; however, every budget includes one or more of the following elements:

- Forecasting of expenditures over a given time
- Cash budgeting (both outflow and net)
- Capital budgeting
- Manpower budgeting
- Variable or flexible budgeting
- Fixed-asset budgeting
- Working-capital budgeting

This chapter will concentrate on cash budgeting and briefly cover capital budgeting and cash flow analysis.

Cash budgeting covers the scheduling of all cash expenditures, showing the amounts needed monthly, weekly, or even daily. The cash budget is one of the DCOM's most important tools. Capital budgeting is the process of planning expenditures for major equipment on which returns are expected to extend beyond one year. One year is an arbitrary but convenient cutoff for distinguishing between kinds of expenditures. Procuring a computer is an obvious example of a capital expenditure, while procuring a complex programming system for which benefits accrue after one year is a less obvious example.

BUDGET COST ELEMENTS

Cost elements that provide a detailed framework for classifying the components of costs incurred by a data center include:

- Personnel related
  —Salaries and wages
  —Other payroll costs
  —Travel, education, and entertainment
- Supplies and services
  —Operating supplies
  —Purchased services
- Equipment related
  —Depreciation
  —Maintenance
  —Hardware rental/lease
  —Software
- Facilities related
  —Building depreciation/rent
  —Utilities
  —Telephone and telex
  —Taxes (all except payroll taxes) and insurance
- Miscellaneous
  —Corporate overhead allocations to the data center
  —Other expenses

The following paragraphs briefly discuss each of these cost elements.

Salaries and Wages. All staff salaries and wages are accounted for in this cost element. Based on the organization's accounting practices, overtime, shift premium, bonuses, and so on are included either in this cost element or in "other payroll costs."

Other Payroll Costs. This element, sometimes known as "fringe" or "benefit overhead," includes such benefit costs as the employer's FICA payments, insurance premiums, and other direct benefits. Vacation and sick leave accrual costs are also included. In most companies this cost element is developed as a percentage of salaries and wages.

Travel, Education, and Entertainment. This cost element includes all costs associated with business travel and entertainment, as well as such education-related expenses as seminar fees and dues for professional associations.

Operating Supplies. This cost element encompasses costs for consumable supplies (e.g., cards, paper, and ribbons); nonconsumable supplies (e.g., magnetic tapes and disks); and general stationery and office supplies. If the corporate central store charges for such supplies, they must be accounted for here.

Purchased Services. Purchased services include expenses for such outside services as keypunch and contract programming; services that can be accounted for under other elements should not be included here. For example, consultant fees for an on-site seminar should be included under Travel, Education, and Entertainment. Certain services may be difficult to categorize. Contracted services for disk cleaning, for example, could be classified under "supplies," "maintenance of hardware," or "purchased services." In such instances the fundamental cost-accounting principle of consistency is the important consideration.

Depreciation. This element includes annual depreciation costs on capital purchases. Depreciation accounting distributes the cost of tangible capital assets, less salvage value (if any), over the estimated useful life of the unit (which may be a group of assets). Guidelines for determining useful life, based on actual experiences of taxpayers, are available from the Internal Revenue Service in Revenue Procedure 62-21. In addition, many organizations have internal guidelines for such calculations.

Maintenance. All costs associated with hardware maintenance, which may include either fixed monthly charges or nonrecurring "time and material" charges, are included under this element. Some rental and lease contracts do not identify a separate maintenance cost; in these instances maintenance costs can be ignored.

Hardware Rental/Lease. This element includes hardware rental and lease charges for all equipment related to DP, including data modems, keypunches, and other support equipment.

Software. This element includes all charges for the procurement and maintenance of software. Some corporations, however, identify some major software as capital assets and depreciate it accordingly. Such software costs are not reflected here but are included under depreciation costs.

Building Depreciation/Rent. Costs associated with the building where the data center is located are included here. Depreciation or rental charges, as well as building maintenance and noncapital improvements, are treated as building costs.

Utilities. All utility costs charged to the data center, including heat, water, and electricity, are identified as part of this cost element.

Telephone and Telex. This element includes costs associated with telephone (voice transmission only) and telex services. Part of these costs may be based on allocations by the corporation.

Taxes and Insurance. All nonpayroll taxes (e.g., property and real estate taxes) are included in this element, as are investment tax credits generated by the purchase of certain capital assets. Costs for all nonpersonnel-related insurance premiums are also included. These premiums usually include policies protecting the building and equipment and may also include premiums for a "disruption of service" insurance policy. In some instances, taxes and insurance charges may be wholly or partly based on corporate allocations to the data center.

Corporate Overhead Allocation. This cost element includes the corporate overhead allocations for corporate services (e.g., personnel and security) that are charged to the data center.

Other Expenses. Any unusual expenses that cannot be directly or indirectly classified under other categories may be identified as part of this cost element.

BUDGET PLANNING

The budget planning process includes the following functions:
- Establishing objectives
- Defining strategies
- Defining policies
- Identifying sequences of events to achieve objectives
- Defining the organization for implementing the plan
- Assuring a review of the budget and an evaluation of feedback

Like many control processes in business and industry, budget planning for the data center should be a closed-loop process. Figure 6-1 illustrates a closed-loop model for budget planning.

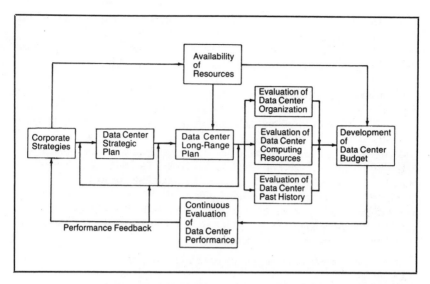

Figure 6-1. Closed-Loop Model for Data Center Budget Planning

The fundamental purpose of budgeting is to assist management in effectively fulfilling two basic functions—planning and control. The following checklist can assist DCOMs in evaluating their own budget planning process:

- Does it force early consideration of the basic policies of the corporation and the data center?
- Does it provide definite identification of responsibility for the functions?
- Does it compel all members of management, from the top down, to participate in the establishment of goals?
- Does it compel management to coordinate data center plans with the plans of other departments?
- Does it force management to clearly identify the resources needed to accomplish the expected results?
- Does it require adequate historical accounting data?
- Does it require management to plan for the most economical use of resources (e.g., manpower, computing)?
- Does it instill at all levels of management a habit of timely, careful, and adequate consideration of all factors before making important decisions?
- Does it help reduce the cost of running the data center?
- Does it provide data center management with a clear-cut definition of plans, freeing time for more creative thinking?
- Does it help communicate basic policies and objectives to the lower levels of data center management?
- Does it help pinpoint inefficiencies and low-productivity areas?
- Does it provide a framework for checking progress or hindrances to progress?

- Does it promote confidence in the ability of data center management to make various business decisions?

The previous checklist may seem elementary; however, many data center managers cannot answer all of these questions in the affirmative.

Budgeting Techniques

For many organizations and data centers, the budgeting process is more an art than a science. Although budgeting for certain cost elements is still somewhat like gazing into a crystal ball, managers should not be misled into believing that this is the only method available. As increasing emphasis is placed on the budgeting process in many organizations, techniques are being developed to minimize the element of guesswork. More econometric models, forecasting services, and economic indicators are being published to assist executives in budgeting. A computer-generated budgeting system, however, is still beyond current capabilities.

Although many variations exist, most budgeting processes fall into one of three categories:
- Incremental budgeting (projections)
- Zero base budgeting
- Baseline budgeting

Incremental Budgeting. In this, the most widely used budgeting method, all cost elements are evaluated with consideration for inflation and changes in corporate and/or data center objectives. For example, if no change is expected in the output of the data center systems group, the systems group's salaries and wages are adjusted for inflation only; actual salaries and wages for the previous period are multiplied by the anticipated average increase in salaries (e.g., 7 percent).

Although this technique is the easiest to use because of its simplicity, it may prove to be the least accurate technique in our quickly changing economy. For example, if a data center budget for the upcoming year has been fixed using an anticipated 12 to 15 percent increase in utility rates, management may be totally unprepared for the 80 to 100 percent increase brought about by such unforeseen circumstances as an oil embargo or economic boycott. Such sharp increases in the cost of one of the cost elements may make it very difficult to manage the entire data center budget. The incremental method of budgeting makes it harder to identify the areas of greatest and least concern to management and provides little information to aid in performing budget cuts in other areas of the data center to compensate for sudden increases in one area.

Zero Base Budgeting. Zero base budgeting (ZBB) assists management in identifying budget areas and expenses and in determining their relative importance in meeting the overall objectives of the data center. Pioneered at Texas Instruments Corporation, zero base budgeting is a simple concept that reverts to management basics. It requires each manager to divide his annual budget into small, understandable components called decision packages. In each package the manager outlines what he wants to do, how he proposes to do it, alternative methods of doing it, how much it will cost, how it will benefit the organization, and what the consequences will be if it is not done. These packages are evaluated in the light of long-range-plan objectives, ranked, and approved to the level of affordability.

Thus, a decision package defines a discrete activity, function, or operation for management evaluation and comparison with other activities.

Since the purpose of a data center is usually to provide services to other departments, these departments will be required to participate with data center management in preparing decision packages. Therefore, a total commitment by the entire corporation and data center management is essential to the success of zero base budgeting.

Baseline Budgeting. Baseline budgeting offers a good compromise to data centers in which total commitment to zero base budgeting is not desired and yet a more formalized budgeting process than incremental budgeting is needed. In this budgeting system, certain baseline budget levels are taken for granted each year, and alterations to these baselines are proposed in the form of small decision packages. For example, the baseline for the data center service level will be determined, and changes in that level will be proposed, along with their impact on the budget. This process is often used by data center managers to justify changes in hardware configuration.

Since an established baseline is usually accepted automatically as a minimum level of service, this method of budgeting inherently restricts a thoughtful, objective evaluation of that minimum level. This method is also less effective in a cost reduction program where even minimum levels must be questioned.

Data Center Budget Development

The data center budget development process will vary depending on the type of budgeting system prescribed by the organization. Accurate accounting data on recent cost performance must be available to data center management to aid in their decision making.

When preparing the budget, managers should consider the impact of many factors on each cost element. The following list includes factors external to the organization, with specific examples that might have an effect on cost elements:
- Sociopolitical environment
  - —Impact of privacy legislation
  - —OPEC decisions
  - —Population migration towards Southwest
- Technology state of the art
  - —Distributed processing
  - —Availability of IBM-compatible mainframes

    —Greater disk density
- Inflation
    —Higher maintenance costs
    —Union agreements
- Scarcity of resources
    —Increased competition for DP personnel
    —Scarcity of paper

Internal factors may also affect cost elements, including:
- Volume changes
    —Increased or decreased processing
    —Increased use of telecommunications
- Application changes
    —Introduction of distributed data entry
    —Planned online purchasing system
- Make or buy decisions (trade-off analysis)
    —Maintenance by in-house staff
    —Forms printed internally
    —Utilization of contract programming
- Productivity changes
    —Productivity aids utilized
    —Learning curve flattening
- Planned events
    —Attendance at seminars
    —Relocation of data center

In addition to these factors, it is essential to gather the statistics that will be needed as a base for most of the decisions. Many of the statistics are used throughout the year for budget control or performance measurement.

The following list includes some of these statistics:
- Employee turnover rate by job classification
- Employee vacation/sick-leave patterns
- Overtime
- Training and development efforts
- Impact of salary administration efforts
- System development versus maintenance versus fix-up time data
- Effect of various productivity tools
- CPU and peripheral times
- Throughput totals
- System response time (e.g., job turnaround time, online response time)
- Number of users and average use time
- Data storage volumes (in all mediums)
- Input volumes
- Output volumes
- System failures—causes and remedies
- Software failures—causes and remedies
- Vendor response time for trouble calls
- Software purchases
- Use of various consumable supplies

- Downtime analysis
- Utility usage
- Telephone/telex use and effectiveness of services

If the accounting system does not provide timely, usable, and accurate statistics, no budgeting system can provide a manager with enough information to serve as a basis for decision making.

COST CONTROL

As stated previously, budgeting includes both planning and control. The effectiveness of good budget planning diminishes significantly if planning is not followed by a good program of cost management throughout the year.

Organizational Involvement

Cost control, like safety, security, and quality, is the concern of the entire organization and not just top management. If all employees are not committed to cost control, top management will find it extremely difficult to institute effective cost-control mechanisms. There are many ways to delegate responsibility for control, ranging from Management by Objectives (MBO), a method that involves assigning total responsibility for cost control to lower levels of management, to implementing organizational policies and procedures for cost control. By instituting a formal MBO system, senior management defines various business objectives and delegates responsibility for achieving them to lower-level managers. Key cost-control parameters can be included in these objectives. The performance of the managers is then evaluated continuously against these objectives.

Presentation of Data

Any budget/finance analyst will agree that it is desirable to break down expenses as far as possible. Presenting this breakdown in a readable, manageable form is also important in assisting cost control at all levels of management. Comparing historical with current data also helps management to perceive cost trends and patterns of spending.

Cost Control for Personnel-Related Costs

In many data centers, personnel costs are greater than all other costs (excluding hardware) combined. Controlling personnel costs involves the following major areas:

- Determining manpower needs
- Recruitment
- Wage and salary administration
- Training
- Job evaluation and planning
- Union negotiations

The most effective tools for controlling personnel costs are timely, accurate reporting of such costs and an ongoing dialogue with all levels of supervision. Consistently competent supervision—direct observation and individual contacts with personnel—is essential for such control. In some instances, comparing standard and actual labor costs may be helpful.

Cost Control for Nonpersonnel Costs

Cost control methods vary greatly, depending on the management style and business practices of the corporation. The following paragraphs discuss some of these methods and their value in budget management. Although used primarily in controlling nonpersonnel costs, these methods are also applicable in controlling some personnel costs.

Authorized Approval Procedure. This is the most widely practiced method of cost control. The data center establishes a procedure requiring each of the expenses and/or commitments for expenditure to be approved by one or more levels of management. Which levels of management are authorized to approve various expenditures is usually determined by the size of the expenditure. Various thresholds are generally established to classify expenditures. In some organizations, certain expenses must be approved by a certain level of management, regardless of their value. For example, in order to control foreign travel, some corporations require that all such trips, regardless of distance or duration, be approved by the highest level of management. Another example is seen in corporations in which a single control is established for all telecommunications expenses, regardless of their origin.

A well-thought-out and strictly enforced procedure for expense authorization will facilitate cost control by creating an atmosphere where expenses are closely scrutinized and budget-versus-expense data is effectively managed. If the procedure is not firmly adhered to, the effectiveness of this form of cost control can be greatly reduced.

Documenting Costs. If costs and cost sources are well documented, future budgeting and cost control will be simplified. Standard forms are often used by corporate data centers to identify and record costs associated with hardware and software. This information is then used to identify and budget hardware rental or maintenance costs and to verify vendor invoices. This type of recordkeeping also assists in asset protection, development of cost recovery (or chargeback) formulas, and resource planning.

Comparison of Standards. To evaluate cost-effectiveness, managers must compare the actual cost with the cost defined as satisfactory or standard. For certain costs (e.g., maintenance costs), standard cost is the cost of the work done by a standard employee with standard resources under standard conditions; for other costs (e.g., travel per diem), standard costs are simply estimates of what is satisfactory. If such standards are used as a cost control method for data center operations, the standard costs must be well thought out and continuously reviewed for applicability. Efforts to measure work performance using standard costs must, of practical necessity, be tempered with common sense; a purely quantitative analysis is insufficient.

Review of Assets and Cost Sources. A thorough, periodic review of assets will assist management in controlling future costs. For example, the development and regular review of a contingency plan will help in controlling the costs of a backup facility. Reviewing the data center security plan can help lower insurance premiums and curb costs associated with theft, fire, and other threats.

ASSET/CAPITAL PURCHASE PLANNING AND CONTROL

Most corporations have a well-defined methodology for planning and controlling the procurement of all assets or capital purchases. Capital budgeting involves generating procurement proposals for such assets as CPUs, peripherals, or the data center building; estimating cash flows; calculating the payback period or return on investment (ROI); approving the procurement; and finally, continuously evaluating the procured asset in the light of the original investment and continuing costs. A procurement proposal is usually evaluated to determine whether it provides a return equal to or greater than the margin required by the organization. In some instances, there may be other factors (e.g., OSHA, EPA, or other legislative requirements) that override consideration of rate return.

Capital Purchase Planning

The following steps are generally followed in capital purchase planning:
- Identification of the capital asset and related procurement costs.
- Determination of the depreciation methodology for the asset. Yearly depreciation figures are utilized in the cash flow analysis.
- Identification of anticipated savings to be realized from the procurement of the asset. Since this is the value that will justify the procurement, care must be taken to identify and cost out all tangible and intangible benefits. For example, when an older computer is being replaced with a newer computer, power and heating savings should also be quantified.
- Preparation of cash flow analysis. The following factors are included in this analysis:
  —Acquisition cost
  —Depreciation schedule
  —Investment tax credit (ITC) where applicable
  —Tax realization from depreciation and ITC
  —Savings generated and resultant tax realization
- Calculation of return on investment and present value of the cash flow.

CASH FLOW ANALYSIS

Since the early 1960s, increasing emphasis has been placed on the management of cash resources. The development of improved cash management techniques is a result of opportunities for increasing returns through higher interest rates (e.g., from time certificates) and programs to improve asset utilization. The organization, in turn, places the burden of managing the cash flow on key components of the business, such as the data center. The purpose of the cash flow forecasting and analysis is to:

- Predict and manage operating cash requirements
- Predict and receive short-term financing
- Predict and select opportunities for cash investment, including the procurement of capital assets

The most common type of analysis used in the data center is the "receipts and disbursements" method. In this method, receipts, whether generated by cash inflow from customer billings or by corporate overhead support, are balanced against the projected disbursements. This method requires accurate planning of monthly cash inflows and outflows and places added emphasis on budget planning. As in long-term financing, capital purchases are judiciously projected through careful estimation of available cash resources.

When planning for cash flows, special attention must be paid to liabilities for payroll taxes if funds from such taxes are invested between the time they are collected and the time they are due to be paid. If there are anticipated inflows from tax considerations (e.g., investment tax credits or depreciation), they must be entered into the cash flow at the date when the savings will be realized (i.e., when the taxes are paid) rather than at the date when the investment is made.

CONCLUSION

The increasing complexity of managerial problems in the data center has led to corporate emphasis on budget planning and control. As DP is beginning to be understood by general management, increasing attention is being given to managing the data center as an operating unit. Efficient operations require careful planning, coordination, and control. In order to keep pace with today's rapidly changing business environment, data center management must chart its course far in advance and use effective budgeting techniques to ensure smooth and efficient data center operations.

7 Justifying the Operations Budget

by Edward J. Kirby

INTRODUCTION

A budget is a plan to assist an organization with its financial management, specifying how much money should be spent for goods and services and when to spend it. Few aids that are as helpful as budgets, however, are as little appreciated by those who use them. Budgets are usually associated with strong negative feelings because there never seems to be enough money allocated. In every organization, managers contend for the same funds, but at the same time, each manager wants to exhibit good fiscal stewardship by containing his own expenses as much as possible.

The DCOM can gain a better appreciation of budgets by referring to current budgets and by maintaining ongoing performance data. When planning to allocate funds, the DCOM might take the opportunity to analyze the impact on performance if more, or less, money is provided for each individual application.

An understanding of fiscal management is essential to the DCOM's approach to budget justification. Budgets should be designed to perform three basic functions. The first and most important function is *control*. Good plans become the standard against which performance is measured and the objective toward which performance is directed. The budget indicates expenditure rates for time as well as money. Any noted variances indicate, if not actual problems, a need for special attention. The second function is *continuity*. A well-prepared budget should communicate information from one manager to the next. For instance, a financial plan facilitates personnel mobility. Transfers, promotions, and increases should not have to be delayed until the end of a fiscal year because of the difficulty in transferring managerial budget responsibility. Incoming managers should be able to understand their predecessors' budgets, given a common method of preparation. The third function is *preparation*. Accurate expense records will keep the DCOM apportion spending for those times most beneficial to the operation, instead of delaying it until money must be spent to avoid a crisis.

THE ROLE OF BUDGET JUSTIFICATION

Ideally, budget justification should consist of an explanation of projected expenses coupled with a prediction of the performance expected (performance is defined here as the benefit users gain as a result of those expenses). Because the goals of the proposing manager and the approving manager differ in emphasis, projected expense requests and explanations must be structured and supported in the DCOM's most persuasive manner. Although both managers are trying to support the organization's objectives, the requester tries to do so by increasing his department's strength, while the approver tries to do so by containing costs.

Financial managers have an interest in both the benefits associated with budget items and in the consequences of not incurring certain expenses. The DCOM should understand that an occasional budget cut will be exercised, not as a personal affront but simply in the interests of good fiscal control.

The defensive method of budget justification is to submit data to management and defend it only when required. The opposite tactic is the positive, offensive approach: prejustification followed by a budget that is accompanied by a statement of the benefits of adopting the budget recommendations. Although this chapter advocates the latter approach, each DCOM must choose between the two approaches with every budget. If the effort of preparing a good offense is neglected, the DCOM, by default, will have to assume a defensive position.

Presenting the Budget

There are three occasions when the budget must be justified. The first is upon identification of a need for either new items or enhancements to old ones. Because this planning stage may be conducted far in advance of the outlay of funds, a written statement should be prepared, containing:
- Identification of the need
- Alternative solutions with associated cost estimates
- A recommended solution with an associated cost estimate
- A recommended time for initiating the solution

This written material should, if possible, be accompanied by an oral presentation.

The second time is the occasion, usually once a year, when appropriations are requested for the forthcoming fiscal period. If no changes have occurred in needs, solutions, or recommendations, reference to the original proposal will suffice.

The third time is when funds are actually committed. It may be necessary to modify previously written statements, but at this point, justification should largely be an oral exercise. Once again, a discussion of changes in needs, solutions, or recommendations is required.

The process and timing of justification may vary between budgets for operating expenses and for capital equipment, since the latter tends to require more attention, emphasis, and advance preparation. The justification technique, however, remains the same; the difference is in the degree of effort required. Recommendations for capital purchases usually are the result of a study, often conducted by an interdepartmental committee. The conclusions of the study should provide the framework for a proposal to management. The lifetime of the equipment should be estimated and the cost indicated by month or by year. Any benefit or cost saving should be charted, indicating the point at which benefits will exceed costs.

BUDGETS: USE AND MISUSE

In order to persuade management of the merits of individual budget items, the DCOM must appreciate the viewpoint of higher-level managers. Above the department level, budgets are used by these managers to predict expenses. Since costs are more predictable than revenues, budgets are the key tool in maintaining a margin of revenue to ensure profits. Corporate-level managers attempt to distribute funds among departments so as to ensure the highest return on investment.

Data center managers may not always have such a functional concept of budgets. Some yield to the temptation to misuse budgets as "wish lists," padding them with extras in the hope that after cuts have been made, at least some will remain. Conflicting motives cause budgets to become objects of contention over which struggles are waged for minor victories.

The corporate manager, too, may have distorted perceptions of the uses of budgets. Knowing that it is his responsibility to take an unbiased economic view of expenses, he may withdraw too far from the details in an attempt to preserve his objectivity. This type of manager demands little explanation of budget items and sees all potential reductions in terms of percentages. There is a danger in this type of approach that the DCOM must avoid. As a manager responsible for providing services to people—services that are performed by other people—being remote or impersonal is an attitude the DCOM cannot afford.

Another misuse of the data center budget by top management is to view it as the *sole* measurement of the data center's performance. This problem is characteristic of some better data centers. Since there may be few complaints or problems by which to judge the center's performance, the DCOM's ability to contain costs may become the only measurable criterion. This management attitude cannot be countered unless the DCOM can provide alternative methods of measuring data center performance.

Setting Financial Objectives

This chapter does not specifically address budget preparation, but there is an obvious correlation between budgets that are well prepared and those that are easy to justify. Good budget preparation means much more than merely inserting appropriate figures on a multiple-column spread sheet. The first step is to set objectives. Some corrective measures for the most common errors in this procedure are separately discussed.

Data center managers often refer to items that have been "buried" in the budget (e.g., a new piece of equipment, a training program for employees, or some aesthetic enhancement of the working environment). Because the DCOM is convinced that if the item were presented directly to management for approval it would be rejected as a frill, he writes it in as inconspicuously as possible and hopes that it will go unnoticed. These support items are as much in the interests of performance improvement as are any others; they are simply more difficult to justify. It is necessary, therefore, to define data center objectives in detail and estimate the resources required to accomplish those objectives.

Providing outside training for an employee is a good example. There is a cost associated with training, travel, and living expenses as well as with the work time that must be covered by someone else during the employee's absence. Employees typically view an outside course or seminar as an opportunity to increase their value and receive correspondingly greater compensation. It provides an escape from routine and a chance to travel, make new acquaintances, and ease job tensions.

To some extent, detailed measurable objectives reveal corporate benefits. The improvement of employee skills by formal training can provide a basis for grading employees at particular skill levels. Direct fiscal benefits can be calculated on the basis of reduced overtime costs substitution, when newly trained personnel can fill in for absent senior skilled personnel, and a decrease in hiring expenses, resulting from strong employee motivation. This goal orientation in the budget presentation or explanation can be a key technique for securing approval.

SELLING THE BUDGET

When the DCOM has an opportunity to present and discuss the budget proposal, he must approach the discussion with an established strategy. The DCOM must identify the item as well as the points that may influence management favorably.

Although maintenance of production rates and the absence of user complaints are certainly indications of a well-run data center, little about them will impress management or attract attention. Are there, for example, any additional services the data center can provide? Can rescheduling or changing priorities increase response times for users who require faster turnaround? Can similar measures be taken to provide greater availability for time-sharing users? Can more or better resources be made available for software development support? The number of skilled employees assuming greater responsibilities can be considered a measurable data center accomplishment in those organizations that define the position of computer operator as a training step to more advanced positions.

Emphasizing Achievement

As a production manager, the DCOM does not personally carry out many tasks. Instead, he controls an operation that, if poorly directed, could cause great problems. Good performance by a production manager is especially impressive if all of the many data center activities are taken into account. The fact that these activities are routine, however, does not mean that they are inconsequential.

The DCOM should develop a list of data center activities and select a few that emphasize the benefits provided by the data center. Such achievements may be:

- Internal training
- Documentation of procedures
- Internal reporting and solution of problems
- Elimination of health and safety hazards
- Improved recordkeeping

Improving Budget Presentation

There are three tools used in budget documentation that help make a presentation to management more convincing. The first is a spread sheet, showing expense distribution and accumulation. Usually, a budget analyst or other representative of the controller's office helps prepare these figures, providing advice on the form and organization of the material to be presented. Consistency with and conformity to organizational standards will make the resulting presentation easier for the audience to read and interpret.

The second tool is the detailed item description. The DCOM should not assume that an item is self-explanatory. The less time required by a manager in asking for explanations, the more time the DCOM will have to present his case. The DCOM should also avoid such descriptions as "miscellaneous supplies" and "casual overtime."

The third tool consists of the facts presented to support item descriptions. Supporting narrative must be tailored to the audience, with items described in terms they can understand. When discussing production, for example, the DCOM should cite items with which management is familiar. He should indicate how services are performed, using the names of those who perform them and those for whom they are performed. Discussions of people should be personalized, using the names of those who will be compensated and motivated by means of the requested budget items.

The proposed budget should not be oversold. Continuing to emphasize the benefits after the item has been accepted may not cause the manager to reverse his decision but probably will not produce a desirable effect.

Classifying Budget Items. In preparing for negotiations, the DCOM should attempt to classify all items of the budget into three categories.

The first category consists of the essential items that make up the basic list. "Essentials" can be defined as items needed for continuous operation.

The second category includes items that appear to be essential but might permit some modification (e.g., deferral of an equipment purchase or a temporary reduction in the inventory of supplies).

The final category offers the greatest challenge to a manager's budget-justification skills. It includes items that only appear to be nonessential. The reduction of many of these items might yield short-term savings; the long-run consequences of such cuts, however, could be critical. Such budget items include equipment overhauls, employee salary increases, and employee training.

It is impossible to enter into any negotiation without being willing to yield on some points. Classifying all budget items will prepare the DCOM to identify items that can be left "on the table" in exchange for concessions by management.

The Negotiation Process

The process of convincing management to accept a proposed budget usually involves preparing written justification and an oral presentation. It is important for the DCOM to be aware that written material must be as persuasive as the oral support. Final budget approvals are usually not given until long after initial submission. Written support ensures that the DCOM's argument will be available until a decision is made.

Strategies should be adjusted to the audience. Managers prefer to hear positive points, improvements, and benefits emphasized. It is crucial, of course, to establish ties between each benefit and the expense necessary to provide it.

If managers tend to view the budget as the sole measure of data center performance and present the DCOM with a proposed budget of their own, the DCOM should direct his presentation toward long-term planning and preparation. He should emphasize the need for contingency resources in case of future crises, the developmental aspects of personnel policies, and the high costs of key employee resignations or massive equipment failures.

When addressing an audience likely to apply across-the-board percentage reductions in the proposed budget, the DCOM can point out instances where small percentage cuts can have disproportionate consequences. For instance, suppose that in a given data center an across-the-board cut of four percent is applied to employee salaries. As there are only 12 employees, the option of eliminating one is not possible. The only possible option for a cut is in scheduled salary increases. It is conceivable that this cut could be implemented without consequence. Should one employee resign, however, the costs of covering the absence, searching for a qualified candidate, training that candidate, and absorbing mistakes until proficiency is attained will probably far outweigh any savings realized by cutting salary increases.

PREPARATION AIDS

The most common difficulty data center managers experience in preparing and justifying budgets is simple discouragement. The work is hard and unfamiliar because the DCOM is more accustomed to managing people than finances. The DCOM may also assume an over-defensive attitude because he lacks confidence in his ability to present his case well.

The DCOM is advised to ask for help in budget preparation. As previously suggested, an internal budget expert is usually available. Other managers with more experience in submitting budgets to the same approving authority can also be of great help.

Perhaps the most valuable (and least used) source of help is user management. While the DCOM can only view the results of service improvements externally, users can specify:
- The benefit expected
- The importance of that benefit
- The dollar value of that benefit

Typically, user management is asked to provide this data for inclusion in a proposal or supporting statement. If user management provides its own supporting documents or oral support, so much the better.

CONCLUSION

The techniques for gaining budget approval are similar to those used in merchandising products and services. Items with market appeal must be identified, advertised, and sold. The DCOM should consider the following guidelines for budget justification:
- Understand the goals of well-prepared budgets: control, continuity, and preparation
- Employ an offensive, not defensive, method
- View the budget as a constructive tool
- Set objectives and orient budget requests toward meeting them
- Establish long-term credibility through accurate reporting
- Search for positive values as selling points
- Apply a personal touch to personnel-oriented discussions
- Be prepared to yield on negotiable points
- Know the readers, and tailor the presentation to their managerial goals, preferences, and habits

Another positive aspect of budget preparation and justification is the repetitive nature of the work. Once it has been handled with a reasonable degree of success, that experience can be applied to future efforts, each of which should be successively easier.

⑧ Evaluating Computer Vendor Support Policies

by the AUERBACH Editorial Staff

INTRODUCTION

Selecting a computer for a specific application or job requires consideration of hardware and software performance. Vendor support services (both pre- and post-installation), hardware maintenance contracts, software maintenance practices, and educational programs, however, may be just as critical to the system's success. Buying a computer based on hardware and software performance alone, without considering other vendor policies, is precarious. This chapter presents pertinent categories for vendor comparison and a vendor questionnaire suitable for evaluating any vendor's offerings. This questionnaire can also be submitted to vendors when a competitive analysis must be performed.

Computer vendors typically market products and services separately. Once the DCOM has decided which hardware and software system is appropriate, careful attention should be paid to available support services and their costs.

EVALUATION METHODOLOGY

For the DCOM to evaluate vendor policies effectively, current information must be available. The checklist in the Appendix can be used to structure the information collection process. The DCOM should first read the vendor questionnaire to become familiar with the specific information used to compare vendor policies and should then choose those questions most pertinent to the desired project or application. Potential vendors should then be asked to respond, in writing, to these questions so that direct head-to-head comparison of answers can be made. If a long series of questions is selected, it may take the vendor representative several weeks to respond, so sufficient time should be allowed in the selection process for gathering this information.

COMPARISON CATEGORIES

Each category of questions in the vendor questionnaire is briefly described in the following sections. The questions presented cover most of the necessary evaluation considerations. All categories may not be needed, since a particular application or user may require only certain types of support. The DCOM may also need to add questions to evaluate a given area in more detail.

Hardware Sales. Policies regarding a manufacturer's pricing structure are one of the primary considerations to be made before purchasing any computer system. This section of the questionnaire contains a series of questions on vendor sales posture, available discounts, trade-in allowances, original equipment manufacturer (OEM) equipment resale, third-party participant (usually leasing company) sales, shipping charges, and delivery schedules. Although this is an important category, pricing and sales policies should never be the sole criteria when a purchase is contemplated.

Hardware Installation. Once a hardware configuration is chosen, attention must be paid to the concomitant installation planning and the amount of support the vendor can actually provide. Facility and site preparation, physical planning, system checkout, and general changes are all extremely important. A competent, cooperative, thorough vendor can usually spell the difference between a relatively trouble-free installation and an installation beset with delays and aggravation.

Hardware Warranty. Another important consideration is the extent and breadth of the hardware warranty. The duration, the types of service included, the charges for the nonwarranted items, and the response of the field service and repair personnel are all extremely important determinants of the quality and usefulness of the warranty.

Hardware Maintenance. After the warranty expires, contract and/or per-call maintenance must be carefully considered in order to plan for most contingencies. The DCOM should understand the types of standard and expedited services available as well as the services that affect different price structures. The availability of maintenance on foreign peripherals is also important, as are the type and cost of maintenance education offered.

Software Products. Software support is also a primary consideration, especially in terms of the cost of license fees and the extent of the license. The form of the software, the updates, and the availability and cost of new versions are critical in choosing a vendor, unless independent software will be developed or purchased.

Software Distribution. The form in which the software is distributed is often important. In addition, distribution media should be convenient and compatible with the DCOM's constraints.

Initial Software Installation. The vendor's professional services are extremely critical to the smooth start-up of a system. Especially important is the length of the warranty period, the status of the software delivered, and the type of personnel responsible for the installation.

Software Maintenance. Once the system is in place, it must be maintained. The types and levels of maintenance, the time frame of maintenance and software fixes, the updates, the cost, and other important software maintenance factors must be ascertained.

Software Education. Software courses are extremely important to ensure effective use of the hardware installation. The availability, cost, and location of the vendor's offerings in software education should be carefully evaluated.

User Groups. Most vendors have user groups to provide a convenient mechanism to share hardware and software experiences. The support of these groups at a national, regional, and local level is important to the DCOM who wants to share common experiences and programs as well as interact with vendor representatives.

CONCLUSION

The vendor questionnaire provides a detailed mechanism for comparing computer vendor policies. Caution must be exercised in using the information, however, because policies vary between corporate and local levels. It is fairly common for a local vendor representative to offer personal enhancements to corporate vendor policies (e.g., providing loaner parts *when available*) if such an enhancement will help to close a sale. These local enhancements are usually promised in good faith, but the local representative may have difficulty in living up to commitments. In these circumstances, it is most important to have the enhancement defined in writing so that the policy is understood by both the vendor and the DCOM. Using this questionnaire properly should guarantee thorough information collection and help the DCOM define the scope and cost of services available.

APPENDIX

Vendor Questionnaire

Hardware Sales

1. Do you rent, lease, or sell your equipment?
2. If you provide a lease, is it a
   - Monthly lease with a 90-day cancellation?
   - One-year lease?
   - Two- to four-year lease?
   - Full pay-out lease?
   - Lease with other terms?
3. Do you offer end users quantity discounts on your equipment?
4. Do you offer quantity discounts to third-party participants (TPPs)?
5. Do you use the same discount schedule for end users and TPPs?
6. What is the range of your discounts for the following quantities?

	End User, %	TPP, %
5 or less		
6–10		
10–19		
20–49		
50–99		
100 plus		

7. Is the discount based on revenue, CPUs, or another variable? Specify.
8. Do you charge separately for:
   - Hardware?
   - Installation?
   - Maintenance?
   - Documentation?
   - Program support?
   - Education?
9. Do you or does the buyer incur shipping costs?
9a. What are your specified delivery times?
   - 30 days or less?
   - 60 days or less?
   - 90 days or less?
   - 120 days or less?
   - 120 days or more?
10. Do you accept trade-in of old equipment on new?
10a. If yes, what is your allowance structure? Specify.
10b. Will you sell used and/or reconditioned hardware?
10c. If yes, how is it discounted? Specify.
11. Will you sell OEM-designated equipment to an end user?
11a. Is the OEM equipment usually sold under your name or that of the OEM? Specify.
11b. Do you sell OEM equipment at the price you paid or at a higher price? If higher, specify the range of markup.

11c. Are there any special charges associated with attached OEM equipment? Specify.

Hardware Installation

12. Is installation included in the hardware price?
12a. If not, what is the charge for installation?
13. What services are included as part of the installation?
  • Physical planning?
  • Facility preparation?
  • Machine replacement?
  • Machine checkout?
  • Software system generation?
13a. Who performs the physical planning?
  • Salesman?
  • Field engineer?
  • Customer?
  • Other? Specify.
13b. What services are included as part of physical planning?
14. Do your installation charges include travel, or is travel additional?
15. In machine checkout, do you use your operating system and a sample program, or do you use diagnostics only?
16. Do you install and check out OEM equipment connected to your system?
16a. If yes, how do you bill for the installation?
  • Included in installation fee?
  • Priced separately?

Hardware Warranty

17. Do you warrant your hardware?
17a. If yes, parts only or parts and labor?
17b. If yes, for what length of time?
  • 30 days?
  • 60 days?
  • 90 days?
  • Six months?
  • One year?
  • Other? Specify.
18. When does the warranty begin?
  • Date of shipment?
  • Date of receipt?
  • Date of installation?
  • Other? Specify.
19. Does customer installation affect the warranty?
19a. If yes, how? Specify.
20. Do you provide warranty service outside of normal working hours?
20a. If yes, is it billable or nonbillable?

20b. Is there an extra charge for weekend repairs?
20c. Do you bill extra for travel?
21. Do you charge for situations in which no defect is found?
22. Do you warrant parts?   ·
22a. If yes, for how long?
  • 30 days?
  • 60 days?
  • 90 days?
  • Other? Specify.
23. Do you repair parts?
23a. If yes, what is the response time? Specify.
24. Do you loan parts?
25. Do you accept trade-in parts?
26. How is attached OEM equipment warranted? Specify.

Hardware Maintenance

27. Do you offer maintenance at the customer's location on:
  • A contractual basis?
  • An hourly basis?
27a. If yes, do you charge extra for:
  • Weekends?
  • Nights?
  • Travel time?
  • Cases in which no trouble is found?
  • Operator errors?
  • Phone-line trouble?
  • User errors?
  • OEM errors?
  • Other? Specify.
28. Is a minimum configuration a prerequisite for maintenance?
28a. If yes, explain.
29. Do you charge to correct a design defect?
29a. If yes, for parts only or for parts and labor?
29b. Is this done on the customer's site?
30. Does your maintenance agreement provide problem determination responsibility?
31. Under your maintenance agreement, do you offer a rebate for extended periods of downtime?
31a. If yes, under what circumstances? Explain.
32. Do you offer expedited service for a premium?
32a. If yes, for how much? Explain.
33. Will you offer a maintenance agreement on an OEM device?
33a. If yes, explain.
34. Will you offer assistance to troubleshoot an OEM device?
35. Do you offer maintenance education?
35a. If yes, is it:
  • Billable and/or nonbillable?

- Available at the customer's location?
- Available at multiple locations? At how many?

Software Products

36. Is your firm's software copyrighted?
37. Do you sell or license your software?
38. Is there a license fee?
38a. If yes, how is it paid?
   - Monthly?
   - Yearly?
   - One-time charge?
   - Other? Specify.
38b. To whom/what is the software licensed?
   - CPU serial number?
   - System? ˉ
   - User site?
   - User firm?
   - Other? Specify.
39. What type of licenses are available to your customers—both end users and TPPs?
   - Object code?
   - Source code?
   - Quantity discount?
   - Secondary license?
   - Unrestricted use?
   - Other? Specify.
40. If an operating system is sysgened on a system different from the one on which it is executed, to which system must it be licensed?
   - Sysgen system?
   - Execute system?
   - Both?
41. If a compiler is licensed and an application program prepared on one system but executed on another, to which system must the compiler be licensed?
   - Prepare?
   - Execute?
   - Both?
42. Is there a fee to execute licensed software on a backup CPU/system?
43. Do you offer software discounts if a customer upgrades from one licensed product to another?
44. Is software under development ever made available to users?
44a. If yes, under what circumstances?

Software Distribution

45. On what media does your firm distribute software?
   - Paper tape?

- Cards?
- Cassettes?
- Minireels?
- Tape cartridges?
- Magnetic tape (7 or 9 tracks)?
- Diskettes?
- Disk cartridges (single)?
- Disk packs (multiplatter)?
- Teleprocessing (communications link)?
- Other? Specify.

46. How is your operating system software delivered?
    - Executable?
    - Object?
    - Source?
47. How many copies of related software publications are provided free with the software?

Initial Software Installation

48. Is on-site software installation service available?
48a. If yes, under what arrangement?
    - Free or part of license agreement?
    - Cost?
49. Who in your firm performs the software installation?
    - Salesman?
    - Hardware customer engineer?
    - Software engineer?
    - Other? Specify.
50. What services are performed during software installation?
    - Unpacking?
    - Sysgen?
    - Backup?
    - Education?
    - Sample program execution?
    - Application design assistance?
    - Application installation?
    - Product problem fixing?
    - Other? Specify.
51. How many days per month is installation service provided?
52. Does the software arrive with all known fixes?
52a. If yes, is it:
    - Preapplied?
    - Ready to apply?
    - Separately obtained?
53. Is the software warranted?

	w/o Installation Service	w/Installation Service
Yes/No?	_____	_____
For how long?	_____	_____
Starting?	_____	_____
What service?	_____	_____

54. What predelivery services are available? What are the associated charges?
    - Applications design?
    - Data center?
    - Application programming?
    - Supervisor modification?
    - Other? Specify.

Software Maintenance

55. Is software maintenance available?
55a. If yes, is it included in the software price?
55b. If it is priced separately, how is it paid?
    - Monthly?
    - Yearly?
    - Other? Specify.
56. Is a hardware maintenance contract a prerequisite for software maintenance?
57. How many types/levels of software maintenance are available? Describe each.
58. When a user sends in a trouble report, by what means is a fix returned?
    - Letter?
    - Newsletter?
    - Phone?
    - On-site aid?
    - Other? Specify.
59. From a user's viewpoint, what is the average trouble report turnaround time?
60. How many months' lapse is there for:
    - Maintenance release
    - New functional version
61. Does the user pay for software functional upgrades?
62. While supported by a maintenance agreement for a typical operating system, what does a user automatically receive from the firm? Specify.
63. What must a user do to receive a new version or release of a product to which he is licensed? Specify.
64. For how many months can a user be covered by a maintenance contract after a new release/version is available if he does not upgrade?
65. What types of on-site assistance/maintenance are available? Specify.
66. Who would perform this on-site software service?

- Salesman?
- Hardware customer engineer?
- Software engineer?
- Other? Specify.

67. What is the fastest way for a user who has a software bug to find out if a fix is available? Specify.
68. If an on-site software maintenance contract is offered, what are the contractual response times (hours/days)?
69. If a user has multiple licenses for the same software product, which of the following are available?
    - Maintenance price discount for each department?
    - A central maintenance plan in which the user maintains a single vendor liaison?

Software Education

70. Does your firm offer software education?
70a. If yes, how is it paid (e.g., fee, credit with license)?
70b. If yes, at how many locations, how frequently, and at what level of detail?

User Groups

71. Do your customers have a user group?
72. Is there a membership fee?
73. Does your user group hold regular meetings?
73a. If yes, how many per year?
    - National?
    - Regional?
    - Local?

⑨ Negotiating with Vendors

by Dale Dull

INTRODUCTION

One of the DCOM's most important activities is negotiating contracts for computer equipment and services; no single activity has more impact on the effectiveness of a data center. Acceptance criteria for new equipment, substandard performance penalties, billing arrangements, and price increase ceilings are only a few of the areas the DCOM must investigate. Even though a vendor may offer verbal assurances of customer protection, the customer's attitude should always be, "Let the buyer beware." This chapter presents a procedure the DCOM can follow to negotiate a contract that will meet his needs and those of his users.

OBJECTIVES OF CONTRACT NEGOTIATIONS

Because the DCOM is responsible for meeting user service requirements, he should have an interest in the equipment and services his users have to work with. The vendor contract defines the responsibilities of and the working relationships between customer and vendor. The DCOM's basic objective in contract negotiations is to arrange a contract he and his users can live with. DCOMs should be aware, however, that they need not negotiate a contract on their own: a team approach can make the negotiating effort more effective. For example, the company's legal and financial departments should be represented on the negotiating team. The legal department team member can provide guidance on contract terminology and legal ramifications of penalties and guarantees. Representation from the financial department is important when deciding whether to purchase or lease, determining break-even points, and performing present-value analyses.

Involving both legal and financial people on the team makes contract review and approval easier once negotiations are completed and an agreement is reached. Since both departments are involved in the entire negotiating process, long contract approval reviews can often be avoided.

In selecting the members for the negotiating team, the DCOM should also consider including one or more of the major users. A team leader or spokesman should be selected to coordinate the various meetings, documents, and follow-up actions. A team comprised of the DCOM, legal and financial department members, and users can give the company a very effective negotiating force.

PLANNING FOR NEGOTIATIONS

The team approach to negotiating can improve a customer's chances for arranging a contract that clearly defines his requirements and provides protection of his rights. While a vendor negotiates many contracts each year, a typical customer negotiates only one contract every five years. It is to the DCOM's advantage to establish a carefully considered plan of attack for the negotiating process. Armed with an effective plan, the negotiating team can be a formidable opponent for even experienced vendors. Another critical element in successful negotiating is allowing enough time for extended bargaining. The time required to complete a contract cannot be predicted; it can take weeks, even months. The difference between successful and unsuccessful contract negotiations can be the team's ability to extend the negotiating process, not yielding on important requirements even when the bargaining becomes tedious.

THE NEGOTIATION PROCESS

The negotiation process should include the following steps:
- Establish the negotiating team
- Educate team members
- Review requirements
- Define strategy
- Schedule and conduct negotiations
- Critique negotiation efforts

Establish the Negotiating Team

After deciding which areas of the company will be represented on the negotiating team, some consideration should be given to selecting a qualified person from each area. Team members should be familiar with DP and interested in getting involved in potentially detailed and lengthy meetings with the vendor. The DCOM can assume the leadership of the team at this stage because of his knowledge of the negotiating process. He should ask potential team members for their help and send formal letters to the appropriate department managers, requesting their assistance.

Educate Team Members

Once the team members are selected, the next task is to educate them. Each team member should become familiar with the goals and objectives of the negotiating process and with DP terminology. Among the sources for this education are:

- Review of the existing contract—The old contract can be used as a model for clauses that should be retained or avoided in the new contract.
- Review of the computer Request for Proposal (RFP)—The RFP defines the requirements of the new system for prospective vendors, who then make proposals offering equipment to meet those requirements.
- Publications on the subject of negotiating computer contracts, such as CNReport, published by International Computer Negotiations Inc.
- Seminars and courses on negotiating.
- Meetings with others who have recently conducted negotiations, especially with the same vendor.
- Review of other contracts to find ideas and clauses that may aid in negotiations.

Review Requirements

At this stage, the DCOM has gone through the RFP process, a vendor has been selected, and formal negotiation is the final activity remaining in the acquisition process. One of the most effective ways to review requirements is to develop a negotiations workbook (see Figure 9-1). The DCOM can develop this workbook and distribute a copy to each team member, ensuring that all team members know the "game plan" and objectives of the negotiations.

Define Strategy

Defining strategy is very important to the overall success of the negotiating effort. The team should discuss the areas listed in the next paragraphs, reach an agreement among themselves, and document the strategy in the workbook.

Objectives. The team members should establish a clear definition, in writing, of exactly what they plan to accomplish through the negotiations, ranking each objective to establish clear priorities. Examples of objectives are:

- Reduce the current lease amount by at least $1,000 per month.
- Establish dollar penalties to be instituted if computer availability falls below 95 percent in any single month.
- Define specific acceptance-test criteria for each piece of new equipment and for the total system.

Prenegotiation Planning. Prior to each negotiating session with the vendor, the team should meet to discuss a plan for that session. Will the team push for a specific concession from the vendor? Who will present which points? Will one team member lead the discussion? At what point should a caucus be called or negotiations suspended? A precise plan is critical to effective bargaining.

Preface
1. General Business Information
   A. Department acquiring system
   B. Key negotiation personnel
   C. Organization chart—DP

2. General Equipment Information and Overall Objectives
   A. Summary of existing DP equipment and other resources (including basic contractual terms)
   B. Summary of proposed DP equipment and other resources (including any suggested trade-in or similar alternatives)
   C. Summary of overall equipment and resource objectives (including replacements, upgrades, time frames, and alternatives)

3. Vendor Information
   A. Name of current vendor; names, titles, addresses, and phone numbers of local and regional vendor personnel
   B. Summary of relationships with current vendor

4. Financial Considerations
   A. Summary of proposed acquisition and financing methods
   B. Assessment of internal rate of return
   C. Existing contract lease credits analysis
   D. Summary of proposed equipment costs

5. Timing Goals and Considerations
   A. Summary of major milestones
   B. Alternative positions

6. Progress on Goals and Objectives
   A. Prioritized goals and objectives
   B. Summary of vendor's inducements and offers
   C. Current estimate of degree to which vendor's inducements and offers meet desired goals and objectives

7. Negotiating Considerations
   A. Assessment of negotiating posture
   B. Expected role of negotiating team, other staff, and experts in the negotiations
   C. Current assessment of possible vendor and equipment alternatives

8. Signature Blocks
   A. Negotiation team
   B. Senior management personnel

9. Contracts
   A. Existing contract
   B. Contract extensions
   C. Model contract and clauses

10. Proposed Contract
    A. Latest draft
    B. Assessment of draft
    C. Problems

Figure 9-1. Negotiations Workbook Table of Contents

Vendor Representatives. The team's success in negotiating depends in part on how well they have assessed the strengths and weaknesses of the vendor. What excites the vendor representatives? How do they work under pressure? Will concessions made at the negotiating table be reversed by the vendor's supervisors?

Post-Negotiation Session Critique. At the completion of each negotiating session, the team should assess the progress they have made. What concessions were given or gained? Are there any items to be followed up before the next session? What are the plans for the next session?

Negotiation Time Frame. Because of the many variables that can affect negotiations, the time frame must be flexible. Ideally, the negotiating team should begin with the understanding that the negotiations will be over only when they sign a contract that is agreeable to them. Not every company, however, has the luxury of prolonging negotiations. In any case, the time frame should not instill in the team a sense of urgency to sign a contract. Such urgency can leave the customer in a weak bargaining position, reducing the chances for vendor concessions.

Ploys and Tactics. Tactics can improve the customer's position. For example, the customer can threaten to call off negotiations and contact another vendor unless the vendor representatives make some concessions. Effective ploys used by customers (and those used by vendors) can be found by reading periodicals and articles on the subject. Other departments of your company that are involved in negotiations are also a source of suggestions.

Contract Items. Specific contract items should be analyzed in order to define a strategy for achieving desired clauses. Although there are numerous contract areas to be addressed, the following paragraphs discuss some of the basic items that the team should focus on.

Payment Terms. The team should define payment arrangements for the equipment. For example, if the equipment is to be purchased, the team could arrange for 75 percent of the purchase price to be paid upon delivery, with the remaining 25 percent paid following a successful 30-day performance period. For a lease arrangement, terms could indicate that payment is to begin the first day of the month following a successful performance period.

Type of Acquisition. There are various ways to acquire a computer system, including purchase, lease/purchase, and lease. Which type is best for each company depends on company policy, cash position, trade-in options on currently owned equipment, confidence in the vendor, long-range plans, and so on. This is an area where the financial expertise of others in the company can be of assistance. Often, vendors offer incentives for one arrangement, according to their marketing strategy. The customer should evaluate the vendor's incentives cautiously.

Delivery Commitments. Often, the only way to make vendor representatives guarantee delivery dates is to include a penalty for late delivery in the contract. A common penalty stipulates that the vendor will pay the scheduled lease payments beginning on the day of promised delivery. Another method is to assess a penalty of two percent of the new lease price for each month that delivery is delayed. Although delivery penalties do not help the company to meet customer needs if the equipment is late, they can provide the incentive for the vendor to keep delays to a minimum.

Acceptance Criteria. Acceptance criteria for new equipment should be tailored to each company's needs. A strictly batch installation, for example, will have different criteria than an installation that also has on-line services. A sample acceptance criterion is a standard of performance under which the customer will use the new equipment for 30 days and achieve an effectiveness level of 90 percent. The effectiveness level can be measured using the following formula:

$$\frac{\text{Effectiveness}}{\text{Level}} = \frac{\text{Operational Use Time Minus Downtime}}{\text{Operational Use Time}}$$

The customer should decide on the minimum amount of operational use time that must be scheduled in a 30-day period to validate the period for the performance test. All special features of the new equipment should be tested and accepted as operable by the customer before final acceptance of the equipment.

Item Position Analysis

As the team discusses the areas listed in the preceding paragraphs, along with many other terms and conditions, they can organize their strategy through an item position analysis (see Figure 9-2). The team should prepare an item position analysis for the most critical areas of the contract. By using a priority rating for each item, the team can define the relative importance of each item in the negotiations. Establishing such a priority system can increase the team's effectiveness in dealing with the vendor. There are many possible priority scales; for example, items could be rated as:

A. Mandatory
B. Highly desirable
C. Optional

Schedule and Conduct the Negotiations

Actual face-to-face negotiations between customer and vendor should be conducted in a businesslike manner, with agendas agreed upon before each session. The customer team, led by one member acting as spokesman, should be in charge of the negotiations and should always follow the prearranged procedure for each session. Because it is critical that proposals be accepted only after careful consideration, the team should not hesitate to caucus at any point during a session to discuss their position on an item. One of the worst mistakes a team can make is to agree to a proposal during a session and then try to change the proposal at the next. It is better to indicate that the team will review the proposed item at a later time before making a decision. Vendors often create a sense of urgency during negotiations to pressure the customer to sign a contract as soon as possible, but the team must resist such tactics and

Item:

Priority:

Name

Date

1. **Item Name:** Trade-in Allowances

2. **Definition:** Amount of money guaranteed by vendor for trade-in of purchased equipment at a future date.

3. **Problem Addressed:** Provide ability to upgrade, downgrade, or delete purchased equipment and receive value for old equipment.

4. **Current Vendor Position:** Negotiable item; no set policy yet, although vendor is working on it.

5. **Contract Solutions:**
   A. Initial Demand(s): Provide contract clause whereby customer has a guaranteed trade-in allowance schedule for upgrade, downgrade, or deletion of purchased equipment, based on the following terms:
      (1) Customer written notice of intent to vendor.
      (2) Declining allowance of two percent of original purchase price per month for the first 36 months following acceptance, with a declining allowance of four percent of original purchase price at the end of each of the next four years, leaving a residual value of 12 percent of original price at the end of seven years.
   B. Fallback Considerations: Could give some on the trade-in allowance schedule of percentages, but a guaranteed trade-in allowance schedule is mandatory for the contract. If percentages are not high enough, work on vendor paying freight charges as an alternative cost savings item.

Figure 9-2. Sample Contract Negotiations Item Position Analysis

take the time needed to obtain an acceptable contract. Once an agreement has been reached between the team and the vendor, formal approval can take place.

Negotiation Critique

When the negotiation process is completed, the team should conduct a critique of their efforts. Items to be reviewed are:
- How effective was the team and the team approach?
- Were original objectives achieved?
- Did the team acquire additional favorable contract clauses as a result of their efforts?
- If the negotiation process were repeated, what changes would the team make?

- Can the experience gained by the team be used to improve negotiations that occur in other areas of the company?

CONCLUSION

The DCOM has a great deal to gain by combining forces with legal, financial, and user personnel in a team effort to negotiate new contracts for computer equipment and services. The different interests and backgrounds of the team members can be coordinated by the DCOM through planning and the use of a negotiations workbook. The result of the team approach will be a contract that allows the DCOM to provide better service to his users.

10 What to Do Before You Call for Service
by Jerry Gitomer

INTRODUCTION

The current vendor attitude toward installation and service—let the customer do it—is a result of the decreasing cost of computer hardware and the increasing cost of labor. In 1955 a computer cost more than one million dollars, and the three full-time customer engineers assigned to each computer installation cost the vendor about $75,000 per year. Today a comparable amount of computing power can be purchased for less than $10,000 (including peripherals), but three customer engineers and the overhead required to support them cost almost $500,000 per year.

With customer engineer assistance now costing $600 per day, significant savings can be realized by the vendor—and passed on to the customer in the form of reduced prices—by having customers install their own equipment. It is expected that by 1990, all but the largest computers will be shipped for customer setup, ready to assemble and plug in. Even now, most vendors insist that customers install their own CRTs, diskette drives, and printers.

Although vendors are concentrating on reducing service costs, they are fighting a losing battle: service operations are labor intensive, computer systems and peripherals are becoming more complex with each generation, and the military is no longer turning out thousands of men with electronics training every year. Consequently, vendors are devoting at least as much design effort (as much as one-third of the electronic circuitry in a system) to reliability, availability, and serviceability as they are to performance. Another way to combat the high cost of service is to use remote diagnostic tools to identify problems. In some cases these tools are automatic to the point where a failing computer is able to dial up the remote diagnostic facility and implement the appropriate diagnostic programs. In most cases today, however, the remote diagnostics require the assistance of a human operator at the site of the failing device. These programs can eliminate unnecessary service calls, and when a customer engineer must make a service call, the right parts and tools are delivered the first time.

Increased service costs, however, are not the sole reason for emphasizing preventive maintenance and user diagnostics. As DP shifts from predominantly batch processing to distributed and interactive operations, the need for a preventive maintenance program becomes crucial. In batch processing, data requires at least one day for turnaround. A system failure corrected on the same day can usually be balanced by a period of overtime work. All the output due the following morning can be delivered on time without any inconvenience to the organization. In a distributed or interactive environment, however, any failure, no matter how small, can interrupt service. For example, the failure of an interactive online order entry system can halt the operations of a wholesaler.

Special Remote Site Problems

Installing terminals at remote sites (e.g., end-user locations) generates another set of problems. As operations personnel at central sites become familiar with equipment, they learn to detect possible sources of failure and to isolate and correct a problem without calling for service. Remote site equipment, however, is not generally operated by DP personnel but by the people in the department where it is located. Operators of this type of equipment are rarely trained beyond learning which button to push to accomplish a specific task. When equipment fails, operators are unaware of the source of the problem or how to search for it. While operations personnel tend to be mechanically inclined and interested in the workings of their equipment, most remote site personnel are not. When remote equipment fails, they simply call for service. Customer engineers responding to these service calls often find that the problems are caused by such simple oversights as improper operating procedures or disconnected line cords.

Besides the differences in personnel attitude and expertise, remote site equipment differs significantly from central site equipment. First, central site equipment provides considerable diagnostic support in the form of operator messages. An operator, seeing a message stating that a disk drive is offline, knows where to begin looking. Remote equipment seldom provides operator messages because it rarely has an operating system. Thus, the remote operator is offered no clues and knows only that something is wrong.

In addition, central site equipment is usually delivered with a complement of aids to isolate a fault. This is seldom the case with remote equipment. Finally, central site equipment failures are generally limited to peripherals; consequently, many installation programs can continue to run, either as is or with minor modifications in job control. When remote equipment fails, however, the entire site is crippled because of the lack of backup hardware. Failures of remote terminals directly affect the customers of an organization. If a supermarket's automated scanning system failed on a Friday night and no one knew how to correct it, it would have an immediate impact on the shoppers.

Because an organization cannot afford to disrupt its employees or customers, the DCOM must work actively to minimize the chances of equipment failure rather than wait passively until such a failure occurs and then call for service.

SEEKING SIMPLE CAUSES

Often a home appliance service call stems from little more than an unconnected plug, a blown fuse, or a tripped circuit breaker; many DP service calls involve problems no more difficult to determine and correct. Unless someone in the installation tries to determine whether a problem has a simple cause that can easily be adjusted by internal personnel, unwarranted service calls and system downtime will continue.

For example, in one installation, the Number 5 disk drive would drop its "ready" status about once every six weeks. This continued for more than a year, and no one could determine the reason. Each time the drive failed, the customer engineer ran all the disk diagnostics and thoroughly tested the drive. It ran perfectly. During each failure, the system was out of service for up to two hours while the customer engineer traveled to the installation and tried to solve the problem.

The cause was finally isolated, strictly by accident, when an operator trainee removed the installation's disk pack so that the customer engineer could mount his diagnostic pack. The trainee turned the pack the wrong way and tightened it. The pack, however, should have been tight already. The problem was that the pack on this drive had never been changed because it was required for only one application; it has been loosening gradually, causing the drive to drop its ready status. The problem was trivial, but until the cause was found, the installation lost more than 20 hours of prime-shift computer time, and the organization lost more than $5,000 in overtime wages to DP and warehouse personnel.

COPING WITH SYSTEM FAILURE

Despite precautions, equipment and even system failure cannot always be avoided. A written procedure should be ready if the system does go down. Separate procedures should be distributed to any remote site. A remote site failure checklist, such as that illustrated in Figure 10-1, ensures that the operator systematically eliminates all obvious causes of the problem. Because many remote site operators are intimidated by the equipment and reluctant to handle it when it fails, the checklist must address the obvious problem areas in a simplified manner.

Local Diagnostic Programs

Assuming that the failure occurs at the central site, the hardware in question should be taken offline and exercised through the controller. A tape drive, for example, can be advanced forward, rewound, and unloaded from the controller. If the item passes these tests, diagnostic programs that will isolate the problem should be run. Only then should the customer engineer be called.

Problem	Possible Causes	Solutions
No operation	Terminal not connected	Plug it in
	Bad socket	Use different socket
	Blown fuse or circuit breaker	Replace
	Fuse or circuit breaker shorts	Repair wiring or circuit
	Fuse or circuit breaker shorts often; overloaded circuit	Use some equipment on different circuits
CRT fan works but not screen	Brightness too low	Turn brightness control clockwise
	Mode switch not on proper setting	Set to half-duplex
	Internal problem	Call for service
Each keystroke appears twice on CRT screen	Mode switch on full-duplex	Set to half-duplex
	Internal problem	Call for service
No communication with central computer	Line switch on local	Set to remote
	Program error	Central operator down-loads program
	Internal problem	Call for service

Figure 10-1. Remote Site Failure Checklist

Remote Batch Terminal Diagnostic Programs

If the failure occurs at a remote site and the failure checklist does not reveal the cause of the problem, the communications controller should be tested to determine whether it is working. If so, diagnostic programs that exercise the remote device from the central site should be run. For a remote batch terminal (RBT), the diagnostics should include transmission of data from the central site to the RBT. The operator should verify that the data was received correctly and directed to the correct device at the RBT. The remote operator should then transmit known test data from the RBT to the central site for each input device at the RBT, and the central site operator can verify the data.

Because most RBT and central site failures are similar for the same equipment types, device diagnostics should then be transmitted to the RBT. The printer test used at the central site, for example, should be transmitted to the RBT for printing. If a failure occurs when remote diagnostics are being performed, the RBT operator should run the same diagnostics in a local mode to determine whether a device failure or a temporary transmission failure is causing the problem. (A device failure will also show when the local diagnostic procedure is run.)

If the system is equipped with remote dumb terminals (nonprogrammable workstation devices), the problem-solving steps for RBTs apply.

Programmable Remote Workstation Diagnostics

Although the programmable remote workstation enables remote equipment to be tailored to the requirements of a specific job and reduces the processing burden on the central computer, it is prone to software bugs as well as hardware problems. The diagnostics for remote intelligent workstations and satellite processors differ from those for RBTs and nonprogrammable devices.

The remote operator should first review the failure checklist to eliminate any obvious problems. The next step is to verify the state of the program in the device. This generally requires the assistance of a programmer familiar with the program. If possible, the best approach is to read the entire memory of the remote device and have it analyzed by the programmer just as a memory dump from the central computer would be analyzed. If the central computer cannot read the entire memory of the remote device, the programmer must teach the remote operator how to display the key areas of the program and data areas. The purpose of this exercise is to isolate the problem without destroying the contents of the remote device's memory so that the remote operator can continue working if the problem is caused by a patchable bug.

Only after all such efforts fail should diagnostics be run. If the local and remote diagnostics execute correctly, the failure is presumably caused by a program bug, which systems and programming staff should try to correct. If they are convinced that the problem is caused by a hardware failure, a service call should be placed.

The Problem Log

For any system failure, the particular problem should be noted in a problem log similar to that shown in Figure 10-2. A problem log should be devised for each piece of equipment and for the installation as a whole. Entries should be made in the log whenever problems occur, even when they are solved by installation personnel.

The problem log should be consulted whenever equipment fails. Besides quickly resolving recurring problems, the log can indicate if any piece of equipment is failing more often than it should. If this situation occurs, the matter should be discussed with the customer engineer. The customer engineer only has the authority to repair equipment and therefore should not be expected to propose that the equipment be replaced or rebuilt at vendor expense.

If the customer engineer cannot correct the problem, management should be contacted. After the problem has been reviewed with the DP manager, a meeting should be arranged with the customer engineer's manager, the customer engineer, and the salesperson.

PREVENTIVE MAINTENANCE

It was once an industry-wide practice for hardware vendors to demand that their equipment be serviced weekly. The customer engineer would arrive at the given installation, clean the tape drives and peripherals, run the diagnostic programs, check the CPU, and inspect peripheral equipment.

Date	Equipment	Problem	Cause	Solution
6/15	Disk No. 1	Water on floor under drive	Cracked hydraulic hose	All hoses replaced
6/28	Printer	Ribbon pulled to left	Broken guide	Replaced
6/29	Keypunch No. 7	No power	Blown building circuit breaker	Shifted to different circuit
7/14	Disk No. 1	Six heads destroyed	Bad pack	Heads replaced, pack removed, other packs inspected

Figure 10-2. Sample Problem Log

Such weekly preventive maintenance is no longer provided; the salaries of customer engineers have made it economically prohibitive. This led hardware vendors to improve product reliability so that such service could be eliminated. Present vendor service contracts are limited to repairing equipment on-site in the event of failure. Depot-only service, however, is beginning to replace on-site maintenance, especially for terminal equipment and the smaller peripherals. Many vendors already service such equipment only at their designated repair depots. This practice is common among microcomputer vendors and is spreading throughout the electronics industry. The IBM Personal Computer, for example, is serviced only at such depots.

One major cause of current computer equipment failure, however, is poor maintenance. Materials strewn around air inlets and exhausts, for example, can lead to premature failure and, in extreme cases, damage beyond repair. If installation personnel fail to clean magnetic tape drives, recording surfaces will erode to the point where tape becomes unusable and read/write heads badly damaged. Failure to change filters on removable disk packs can lead to contamination of recording surfaces and disk head crashes, resulting in the loss of a mounted disk pack and damage to disk drives. The printer, card reader, and card punch should be vacuumed to prevent buildup of paper dust that can abrade machined surfaces. The manuals supplied with peripheral equipment specify the maintenance required and usually include detailed illustrations. These instructions should be followed carefully.

Frequently equipment will give an early warning of possible failure; this is especially true of mechanical components. A change in the sounds of the equipment operating is a common warning signal. If such a change occurs, the customer engineer should be contacted. Test decks, tapes, disks, and a series of programs can often help to indicate a problem.

Maintenance Aids

To work on equipment, the customer engineer must be able to gain access to it. If supplies are stacked behind peripherals and materials are piled on top of equipment cabinets, the engineer cannot work freely. Although many engineers move away such materials themselves, they are not obligated to do so. The time lost in moving obstacles is even more important. The engineer cannot start working until all obstacles are cleared.

Frequently, considerable time can be saved by carefully describing the problem by telephone before the customer engineer comes to the installation. The engineer may be able to define the problem area enough to be able to bring the required parts and specialized test equipment on the first trip. This can be a particular time-saver in a busy metropolitan area if the engineer can avoid any return trips to the office.

CONCLUSION

The impact of equipment and personnel problems can be reduced if the DCOM organizes and staffs a failure-prevention program that establishes various points for examining and auditing hardware and software as well as their related controls. Such diagnostic problems should be incorporated into overall operations procedures; special emphasis should be placed on training remote site operators to follow a simple checklist when equipment fails. Testing first for the simplest cause of failure and proceeding to increasingly complex causes will eliminate unnecessary service calls. In addition, personnel should adhere to strict maintenance procedures. In today's complex business environment, service personnel, time, and money are already too scarce to waste on problems created by poorly maintained equipment; these preventive measures will help the DCOM reduce such expenditures and maintain uninterrupted operations.

11 Separation of Duties in the Data Center

by Bryan Wilkinson

INTRODUCTION

The separation of duties is a long-standing organizational technique used by accounting departments to ensure proper control. An understanding of the accounting principles behind the technique can help the DCOM to apply it in the data center.

The American Institute of Certified Public Accountants (AICPA) issues various Statements on Auditing Standards (SAS). SAS No. 1 defines *incompatible functions* (i.e., duties that are not properly separated, resulting in loss of control) as follows:

> Incompatible functions for accounting control purposes are those that place any person in a position both to perpetrate and to conceal errors or irregularities in the normal course of his duties. ["Errors" refers to unintentional mistakes, and "irregularities" refers to intentional distortions of financial statements and to defalcations (acts of embezzlement).] Anyone who records transactions or has access to assets ordinarily is in a position to perpetrate errors or irregularities. Accordingly, accounting control necessarily depends largely on the elimination of opportunities for concealment. For example, anyone who records disbursements could omit the recording of a check, either unintentionally or intentionally. If the same person also reconciles the bank account, the failure to record the check could be concealed through an improper reconciliation. This example illustrates the concept that procedures designed to detect errors and irregularities should be performed by persons other than those who are in a position to perpetrate them—i.e., by persons having no incompatible functions.

The definition refers to accounting control, and the example given is a manual procedure not involving DP. The DCOM may ask what this has to do with DP operations. SAS No. 3 explains the relevance:

> Frequently, functions that would be considered incompatible if performed by a single individual in a manual activity are performed through the use of an EDP program or series of programs. A person having the opportunity to make unapproved changes to any such programs performs incompatible functions in relation to the EDP activity.

Thus, anyone who can access and make unauthorized changes to operational programs is performing incompatible functions.

SAS No. 3 next defines supervisory programs as operating systems and data management systems, and it states:

> An individual who can make unapproved changes in supervisory programs has opportunities to initiate unauthorized transactions that are like those of a person who can make unapproved changes in application programs or data files; he therefore performs incompatible functions.

Thus, the software programmers, the data base administrator, and perhaps others are in a position to perform incompatible functions.

To ensure that no one in the data center is overlooked, SAS No. 3 continues:

> EDP personnel have access to assets if the EDP activity includes the preparation or processing of documents that lead to the use or disposition of assets.

Since processing data about assets (e.g., money and inventory) is the primary function of business DP, everyone in the data center has access to assets and is in a position to "perpetrate errors or irregularities."

To minimize exposure to errors and irregularities, SAS No. 3 stipulates that compensating controls be applied. Examples of compensating controls are limitations on access to the equipment and to the data library, effective supervision and rotation of personnel, and use of document counts and control totals.

Acceptable controls are required by law as well as by the AICPA. In 1977, the Foreign Corrupt Practices Act was passed. It requires all companies registered with the Security and Exchange Commission (SEC) to adequately maintain a system of internal controls. These controls must ensure that transactions are properly authorized and recorded and that the company's assets are safeguarded.

One recognized and proven control is the separation of duties. If there were no auditing or legal requirement for the separation of duties, the DCOM would still have an interest in separating responsibilities in order to increase the security of the DP operation. If duties are separated, access to the computer, the data library, and the programming documentation can be limited and the potential damage from the actions of any one person reduced.

DEFINING THE NEED FOR SEPARATION

Auditing standards call for complete segregation of functions; for example, only operators should have access to the computer, only the librarian to the data library, only programmers to the application system documentation. Unfortunately, this is not always practical. In a small shop, the manager may also act as the programmer and the backup operator. The data entry supervisor may serve as the control clerk. There may be no data librarian, this function performed instead by the operator. In the interest of economy, even large organizations may combine such functions as data entry and control or computer operations and maintenance of the tape library.

Some functions are separated "naturally" for reasons other than control and security. It is not cost-effective to have a high-priced programmer enter data or run production jobs on the computer. In some cases, however, necessary job separation is not economically justified. For example, it might be cost-effective to have programmers operate the computer when testing their own programs; however, from a control standpoint, the programming and operating functions must be kept separate.

Cost and Separation of Duties

If the DCOM looks only at costs versus benefits when making organizational and operational decisions about separation of duties, a particular cost should not be overlooked: the expected loss resulting from combining duties. This cost can be estimated, although roughly, through risk analysis.

In risk analysis, the expected loss of a company equals the potential loss resulting from an undetected error multiplied by the probability of such an error, plus the potential loss resulting from an irregularity (a defalcation) multiplied by the probability of such an irregularity. With an accounts receivable system, for example, the potential loss from undetected errors might be $50,000 a year. The probability of such losses might be 0.05. The potential loss from irregularities might be $1,000,000 (not unusually high for a computer crime). The probability of such a loss might be 0.002. The expected loss in the accounts receivable system would then be ($50,000 × .05) + ($1,000,000 × .002) = $4,500. If similar figures are developed for all other applications, the sum of these figures is the expected loss to the company of operating without adequate controls—including separation of duties.

Although the potential losses and the probabilities are only rough estimates, errors, irregularities, and losses do occur, and the possibility of these problems should not be ignored. When performing a risk analysis, the DCOM should work with the controller and the auditors to develop reasonable estimates of probabilities and expected losses. The total expected loss should be compared with an estimate of the loss that can be expected even if controls are put in place. The difference between these two figures is the true cost of not having controls.

Another factor that should be considered in a cost/benefit analysis is the personnel cost involved in separating duties. If duties are properly segregated, it may be necessary to increase the staff because one person cannot perform functions that are separated. This increases salary and benefit costs. With proper scheduling, however, these costs can be minimized by using part-time personnel.

Another potential cost of separating duties is loss of morale because of restrictions regarding on-the-job training for upgrading employees. A control clerk cannot be given on-the-job training in computer operation while also working as a clerk. A computer operator must be discouraged from learning programming. An application programmer must be dissuaded from learning systems programming.

Alternatives to Separation of Duties

When analyzing the need for separation of duties, the DCOM should consider other techniques that can minimize undetected errors and discourage irregularities. The most acceptable technique is close supervision, although this also has costs. Careful review of inputs, outputs, console logs, and source listings; on-the-floor observations of personnel; random inspections of work being done; and discussions of actions and decisions with the staff—such techniques catch errors and reduce irregularities.

Another useful technique is to build adequate controls into all systems. For example, all important data fields should have programmatic edits; money fields should have limit and/or reasonability tests. Exception reports, transaction lists, master file change reports, and master file listings should be prepared by all systems. In addition, batch systems should provide batch balance reports and error listings. Control totals and record counts should be created and verified by the first program in a system, and these totals should be passed from program to program and be reverified. Operator interventions should be held to an absolute minimum.

Two types of packages on the market provide some assistance in maintaining control. A tape management system reduces the need for a tape librarian and decreases the possibility of unauthorized changes to data files. Program management systems that protect production programs from "on the fly" changes and that create an audit trail of all program changes provide an operational control in the programming area.

When a data center has two or three shifts, rotating personnel between shifts provides a measure of control. Of course, when shifts are rotated, the manager should ensure that the applications are not rotated also. If a data entry operator or computer operator knows that someone else might work with an application, the temptation to perpetrate irregularities is reduced.

In summary, when the DCOM is deciding whether functions should be separated, he or she must consider:
- The size of the operation. (The smaller the staff, the harder it is to separate functions.)
- The risks involved in not separating duties.
- The potential costs of segregating duties.
- The possibility and the advisability of using alternative techniques to achieve the same measure of control.

FUNCTIONS TO BE SEPARATED

The following job functions should be studied for possible separation:
- Control clerk
- Computer operator
- Data (tape) librarian
- Data entry operator
- Systems analyst/application programmer
- Systems programmer
- Data base administrator
- Security administrator
- CRT operator in the user area
- User providing batch data
- User using output
- EDP auditor

The following paragraphs list the duties that can and cannot be performed in each job function if proper separation of duties is to be maintained.

Control Clerk. The control clerk serves as a switching center for the operations group. In installations where data is entered by the users, the control clerk logs batch numbers, counts, and control totals before giving the data to the operators. If the DP department is responsible for data entry, the control clerk logs the same information and then turns the input over to the data entry section.

After the input is keyed and verified, the documents and the machine-readable input are again given to the control clerk, who logs the input and forwards it to computer operations. The documents are checked against the batch log and returned to the users. Control receives all output from computer operations, logs it, and verifies run-to-run controls. Errors, exceptions, and out-of-balance batches are logged to ensure that they are corrected in a timely manner by the users. The control clerk may or may not handle the distribution of output. Since control monitors the activities of the computer operations group, the control clerk should not report to the manager in charge of computer operations.

Computer Operator. The operator runs the computer for both production and testing and may pull and refile tapes if the company has a tape management system. If the operating system does not keep a record of operator actions, the operator logs the time of job starts and completions, operator actions, and operator interventions. The operator does not have access to control totals and is not permitted to enter or change data on any file by making a console entry.

Data (Tape) Librarian. The librarian pulls and returns all files, checks all operator-applied external labels, and maintains proper file backup, both on- and off-site.

Data Entry Operator. This employee keys and verifies input but does not verify his or her own work. The operator corrects data entry errors but does not initiate other input or correct other errors. If the equipment permits, the data entry operator enters and verifies batch totals and batch counts.

Systems Analyst/Application Programmer. This employee designs and programs new applications, performs program maintenance, and documents these activities in accordance with department standards. (In some organizations this function is shared with a documentation specialist.) The programmer/analyst also works with users to develop test data. This employee does not run the computer; does not provide input to production systems; and does not make revisions to the operating system, the data base management system, the communications controllers, or other technical software.

Systems Programmer. This employee does maintenance and enhancements for all technical software, documents all changes, and provides assistance for unusual computer failures and aborts. The systems programmer does not work on application programs and does not run the computer when live data files or production programs are mounted.

Data Base Administrator. The DBA establishes procedures for the daily operation of the data base and the DBMS and ensures that they are followed. This employee also adds new elements to the data base and modifies logical relationships as necessary; develops, maintains, and controls the data dictionary; and works with programmers and users to develop test data that properly represents the data base. The DBA reports directly to the head of DP.

Security Administrator. This employee assigns, changes, and controls passwords; works with user management to determine access limitations for files and data fields and implements these limitations through password and/ or terminal access controls; and works with DP management to determine access limitations to programs and implements these limitations through password controls. The security administrator also ensures that data is encrypted as necessary, ensures security of password tables (machine readable or hard copy), and investigates actual or attempted security violations. The security administrator reports either to the head of DP or to the DBA.

CRT Operator in the User Area. The terminal operator enters data directly onto files from source documents or from telephone communications and corrects data entry errors online. If data is entered from source documents, the terminal operator batches and develops control totals. Batch counts and control totals are checked against batch balance reports by someone other than the operator entering the data.

User Providing Batch Data. The user batches source documents, develops batch counts and batch totals, and checks these against batch balance reports. The user also reviews error reports and corrects input errors. (Whenever a user corrects his or her own batch total errors and input errors, the errors and the corrections are reviewed by a supervisor.) Exception reports (e.g., items that exceed predetermined limits) are always reviewed by a supervisor, rather than by the person providing the exceptional input.

User Using Output. The user reviews and approves the design of reports, assists in developing test data, and logs all reports to ensure that they are received.

EDP Auditor. (There is little agreement within the profession regarding the extent of audit involvement in system design. A suggested approach follows.) The auditor develops standards for control and audit trails that should be incorporated into system and program designs. The auditor also reviews design documents and completed systems to ensure that they adhere to the standards, develops standards for administrative and operational controls, and periodically reviews the DP operation to verify adherence to standards. The EDP auditor is not part of the DP department.

HOW TO ACHIEVE SEPARATION

There are various ways to achieve separation of duties, some of which have been discussed: through organizational structure, technical means, physical measures, and administrative practices. None of these approaches can work alone; they should be combined to achieve proper segregation of functions.

Organizational Separation

The most obvious and most widely used technique for achieving separation of duties is placing incompatible functions in different organizational areas (e.g., programming and computer operations can be organizationally separated). For organizational separation to work, every employee must understand how the functions are separated. This understanding can be achieved by using job descriptions, perhaps supplemented by organizational charts. One of the major considerations when using organizational separation is that two organizational units should not be responsible for the same function. Besides complicating the separation of duties, dual responsibility makes it more difficult to establish accountability.

Some guidelines for organizational separation are:
- Control functions (listed earlier) should not be split (e.g., between data entry and control).
- Since control monitors the activities of computer operations and data entry, it should be organizationally separated from them.
- The operations supervisor should not have responsibility for systems and programming, nor should the systems and programming supervisor have operations responsibilities.
- The systems and programming supervisor should not have responsibility for or control over data entry.

- The systems programmer should not report to the systems and programming supervisor.
- The data base administrator should report to the head of DP.
- The security administrator should report to the head of DP or to the head of data base administration.
- The EDP auditor should not be part of DP.

Technological Separation

Technology can assist in separating functions through various software packages. Three useful types of packages are tape management systems, program management systems, and security packages.

Tape Management Systems. Tape management systems allow tape libraries to be run using only a number for the external tape label. With such systems, the content of a file cannot be discovered without a library listing. This limits access to assets. For example, it would be next to impossible for someone without a library listing to make an unauthorized copy of a personnel file. Even after gaining access to the library, it would be impossible to discover which of the hundreds of tape reels held the personnel file.

Program Management Systems. Program management systems (PMSs) discourage irregular alterations to programs by providing an audit trail of program changes. Another function performed by many PMS packages is preventing changes to live production programs—another limitation on access to assets.

Security Packages. Security packages are another technological method for separating functions and limiting access. Through proper password procedures, for example, programmers can be denied access to live data files, and users can be denied access to programs. Thus, programmers cannot enter data, and users cannot change programs. Separation can also be carried one step further: user access can be limited to specific files, and programmers can be given access only to programs for which they have responsibility.

Security packages perform other functions in addition to password control. They can keep a record of log-on violations and can disconnect a terminal after a predetermined number of successive log-on errors. This prevents an unauthorized person from gaining access to files and/or programs through trial and error. Security packages can also record illegal requests and alert the security administrator so that an immediate investigation can be made. In addition, the packages can log all file accesses (or only accesses to restricted files) in order to facilitate investigation of unauthorized changes to these files.

Physical Separation

Separation of duties can be implemented and enforced by physical means; for example, physical access to the computer should be limited to computer operators, operations management, and field engineers (field engineers should be accompanied and closely observed by operations supervision). Physical separation can be enforced by placing the computer in a room with locked entrances or by using guards and badges. People who need access to the computer room, but not to the computer, can be issued badges that authorize access at particular times or under certain conditions. In this category are the tape librarian, janitorial staff, EDP auditors, and possibly control clerks.

Tape Library. If a tape management system is not used, access to the tape library must be limited in some other way. Only the tape librarians and their supervisors who do not operate the computer should have access. This limitation can be enforced by locating the tape library in a separate room adjacent to the computer room. The door between the computer room and the tape library should be locked.

Terminals. With the advent of RJE and online terminals, physical access to the computer is no longer needed to use its programs, files, and computing power. Thus, RJE and online terminals should also be protected from unauthorized access. RJE terminals should be placed in locked rooms. This may be impractical for online terminals; in such cases, terminals equipped with locks should be used. In addition, the communications systems that control online terminals can limit the hours of use (e.g., from 8:00 A.M. to 12:00 P.M. and from 1:00 P.M. to 5:00 P.M.). Passwords and/or machine-readable badges can also be used to limit access to terminals.

Program Documentation. As programmers should not have access to the computer, operators should not have access to program documentation that would enable them to understand, and thus modify, a program's functions. Furthermore, programmers should not have access to the documentation of programs for which they are not responsible. To ensure this type of separation, program documentation should be physically controlled. It should be kept in a central location where it can be locked up when not in use, and checkout procedures should be used. These physical controls are important for both programs in production and programs under development.

Employee Seating. Finally, persons performing similar functions should sit in the same area. Conversely, the seating arrangement should not intermix people performing incompatible functions. This physical separation simplifies the security aspects of the supervisor's task.

Administrative Separation

Many administrative rules or actions can be used to achieve separation of duties; including the following:
- All tests should be run by computer operators.
- Live data files should never be used for test purposes.

- Users must participate in the development of test data.
- Check stock and other negotiable paper should be stored, controlled, and accounted for by someone not in the DP department.
- All negotiable paper should be numbered, and its use should be logged.
- All runs involving negotiable paper should take place on weekday shifts. Two people should be present during the runs.
- Computer operators should not have access to control totals.
- DP personnel must not originate entries for processing.
- Runs of specific applications should be rotated among operators on a basis unknown to the operators.
- The keying of input to a given application should be rotated among data entry operators.
- All DP personnel should be required to take annual vacations, at least five days of which should be consecutive.
- All errors, except keypunch errors, should be corrected by users. If a user corrects his or her own errors, the errors and the corrected values should be reviewed by a supervisor.
- Data entry operators should not verify their own work.
- Control personnel should ensure that all errors are corrected by users, either by keeping a copy of all error, exception, and batch balance reports or by logging errors.
- All systems designs should be approved by users and EDP auditors.
- All documentation should be reviewed by supervisors to ensure adherence to standards.
- Console logs or reports should be reviewed by supervisors to detect unauthorized actions and interventions.
- Security reports produced by the security package or other software should be reviewed by the security administrator to detect unauthorized accesses and actions.
- Reports produced by the program management system should be reviewed by program supervision to detect unauthorized program changes.

IMPLEMENTATION ISSUES

Implementing measures to ensure separation of duties can cause problems. The following paragraphs discuss some of the issues that should be considered so as to minimize these problems.

Personnel Problems

Personnel difficulties are the greatest obstacle to implementing a program of separation of duties. It is necessary to tell employees that they can no longer perform some tasks they are used to performing—tasks that they may have assumed were part of their duties. An operator, for example, may have to be told that all dates, beginning check numbers, and so on will be entered through JCL rather than from the console. Such changes may make employees feel that they are mistrusted or that their jobs have been downgraded.

The DCOM must allay these fears and explain that the purpose of separation of duties is to protect the employees and the company. As a last resort, the separation of duties can always be blamed on the auditors; most auditors are happy to shoulder the blame if the result is improved control.

On-the-Job Training. As previously discussed, strict adherence to separation of duties complicates on-the-job training for upgrading purposes. One way around this problem is a clean cutover from job to job. If an operator wishes to be a programmer, then he or she should be relieved of operator duties and should become a full-time programmer trainee.

Emergencies. Special provisions regarding separation of duties must be implemented in emergencies. For example, if the department is short an operator and a programmer knows how to run the computer, it may be necessary to violate strict separation standards for short periods of time. This can be compensated for by closer supervision and closer review of control reports. Procedures adopted in emergencies could become accepted methods of operation; however, "emergencies" that last more than two weeks should be treated in other ways—for example, by hiring a temporary employee.

Enforcing Separation. Separation of duties is enforced by supervision. Written job descriptions and written standards must be established, communicated to the employees, and enforced by the supervisors. Managers must appropriately discipline employees who break the rules.

CONCLUSION

The DCOM should develop a set of job descriptions that ensure that no two organizational areas have responsibility for the same functions. The duties of a given job should be structured so that no person is in a position both to perpetrate and to conceal errors or irregularities in the normal course of duties. The job descriptions should be supplemented by a set of standards. The standards included in this chapter can be used as a starting point.

If the organization lacks technical aids (e.g., tape management systems, program management systems, and security packages), they should be installed. If such aids are being used, they should be reviewed to ensure that all needed control features have been implemented. A program for regular review of the control reports produced by these aids should be instituted.

The organizational structure should be reviewed to ensure that it encourages strict separation of functions. If it does not, the structure should be revised.

Physical security should also be reviewed. If locks, badges, or walls are missing, plans should be made to acquire them.

Finally, the staff should be told about the separation-of-duties program. The importance of the program should be emphasized, and written job descriptions and standards should be made available to all employees.

The DP operation is becoming more and more important to auditors. The Foreign Corrupt Practices Act is an example of the increased emphasis on requirements for effective systems. Separation of duties and control over access to assets are time-honored and proven methods of control. The DCOM should take the lead in implementing such controls.

12 Selecting Data Security Software

by Robert W. Edwards

INTRODUCTION

In recent years, the DP community has realized that the security and privacy controls offered by the systems software of most third-generation computer systems do not meet current and future needs. Several vendors have developed software packages designed to enhance existing security controls or to provide additional protective measures. The prospective user of these packages faces a bewildering array of conflicting claims and computer security jargon. To ensure that an organization acquires the right security software package for its needs, it is essential that the potential user know how to define system security requirements, establish technical evaluation criteria, identify potential software packages, and conduct a product evaluation.

DEVELOPING DATA SECURITY CRITERIA

The first step in selecting data security software is to gain a clear understanding of what the software package must do to meet the organization's needs. A software security package is only one component of an overall DP security program. For this component to be effective, it must be carefully integrated with the other components of the security program (e.g., physical security, personnel security, hardware integrity, contingency planning). All too frequently, DP managers think that a security software package can provide total protection; this leads them to neglect other critical elements of the DP security program.

To avoid this mistake, the potential user of a security software package must clearly understand:
- The level of security required and the role to be played by the security software in maintaining this level
- The relationship between the security software and other existing or planned elements of the DP security program
- The functional, technical, and administrative criteria for selecting a security software package

This chapter addresses the third issue—the functional, technical, and administrative criteria that must be established in order to identify, evaluate, and select a security software package.

Functional Criteria

Regardless of the system or information to be protected, the selection of a security software package must be based on its ability to support certain administrative objectives, which can be divided into four categories:
- Accountability
- Auditability
- Integrity
- Usability

These same categories are universal criteria for the design, development, implementation, and maintenance of all reliable software and systems. When applied to data security software, however, these criteria become especially critical. It is the responsibility of both executive and line DP management to determine the control limits for each of the four categories and to obtain the most viable protection package possible.

Accountability. This key functional area involves the means by which individual users of a system are held accountable for their actions. To provide accountability, a security system must be able to positively associate a process with its source of authorization. DP management must determine the following when considering accountability criteria:
- Individual accountability for all system-related actions—Each transaction or job must be associated with an individual or, in the case of production jobs, with a department or application. Since production jobs usually access more sensitive data than do individual user's jobs, controls must be available to ensure that a user's job cannot obtain production identities.
- Control of access to resources—Resources that can be controlled by security software include data sets, transactions, TSO account numbers, TSO procedures, batch account numbers, and project control numbers. A security system must be flexible and extensible so that new resources can easily be defined and controlled.
- Specification of the manner in which resources are accessed and manipulated—Frequently, resource-level controls are inadequate to provide full protection. In such instances, the access method itself (e.g., program or transaction) becomes vital in determining access permission. Security software makes use of such variables as input device, terminal location, access date and time, and job input source to specify and limit access to resources. Implicit in the use of such a security system is the determination of users responsible for each group of data.

Auditability. In general, auditability is the ability to produce regular audit trails and reports to show who accessed and manipulated what resources. It is also desirable for some systems to record how and by whom *access control* information is modified. Therefore, all updates to the security system's control data base should be closely monitored. In determining criteria for the

selection of security software, management should evaluate at least the following:
- Access logs—Record who accessed what.
- Violation logs—Record who attempted what.
- Modification logs—Record who changed what.

Integrity. This is a measure of how easily a system can be circumvented. A data security system that has integrity is thorough, consistent, and complete. Management must consider the number and nature of the functions that a data security system monitors when evaluating their organization's requirements. Typical access functions that may be monitored are:
- Allocate
- Open/EOV (for Read/Write Execute)
- Scratch
- Rename
- Catalog
- Uncatalog
- Recatalog

It is equally important to evaluate the degree of protection provided if the data security system should become disabled. Recovery procedures should be examined for security checking (manual and/or automatic), audit capability for all system interactions, and controls over use of duplexed copies of files or backup tapes.

Usability. The fourth critical factor in the selection of a security software package is usability. Two elements—human factors and costs—should be considered when developing functional criteria in this area.

Human Factors. While providing the levels of accountability, auditability, and integrity necessary to meet an organization's security requirements, a security system should not impose unacceptable constraints on system users. Users who feel that the restrictions imposed by the security system are unnecessary may try to beat the system, thus negating a great deal of its effectiveness. It is also important to not go too far in the other direction, however. Security systems that emphasize user friendliness may, in fact, provide very little protection. There is an unavoidable trade-off between total system security and user friendliness—DP management must develop a set of functional requirements that balances the advantages of these two factors as much as possible.

Cost. Both human and machine costs must be evaluated for installation, implementation, operation, and maintenance. In evaluating security systems, cost/benefit relationships must be closely examined. The system must be designed to minimize the use of personnel resources and to keep the consumption of processing resources within acceptable limits. It is also important to evaluate both recurring costs and costs incurred only at the time of implementation.

Technical Criteria

After establishing the functional and operational requirements that the software must meet, the user must establish the technical criteria for selection. These requirements are a function of the specific hardware, software, and telecommunications environment. The proper definition of this environment is critical to the selection of an effective security software package.

Compatibility. The most significant technical criterion that must be met by any proposed package is compatibility with the existing or proposed hardware, software, or telecommunications configuration. No matter how effective a package may appear, if it requires extensive hardware or software modifications, it should be eliminated from consideration.

Hardware Compatibility. The first compatibility issue is the package's ability to perform (without major modifications) on the target hardware architecture. Many packages have been developed by vendors for use only on specific hardware systems. For instance, RACF (IBM) and ACF2 (Cambridge Systems Group) are designed for implementation on IBM systems, while the MULTICS operating system will only operate on Honeywell hardware. The user must define the architecture of the target system (including any proposed hardware modifications) and establish minimum acceptable performance standards that the proposed security software must meet.

Software Compatibility. A more difficult issue is software compatibility. The question of hardware compatibility is essentially binary—the target hardware either will or will not support the proposed software. In the case of software, however, the issue is often far less clear. A number of issues must be considered when developing selection criteria based on software compatibility:

- Systems Software—Although different packages may be capable of operating under a particular operating system, DBMS, and/or communications package, their performances in the same software environment may differ considerably. A good illustration of this is the different performance characteristics of ACF2 and RACF when operating in the same IBM System/370 MVS environment. Table 1 lists some of the differences between the two packages.
- Applications Software—The proposed security software should also be compatible with the installation's applications systems. The user should carefully evaluate the impact of security software on these systems. Among the areas that should be considered when developing technical criteria in this area are:
  - —Data Structures. Will the proposed security software require modifications in files, data sets, or other data structures?
  - —Processing Routines. Will the proposed software affect processing routines and data flow in existing applications systems?
  - —User Access. Will the proposed software adversely affect the user's ability to access critical data or processes necessary for the successful performance of an operational function?

Table 1. Functional Comparison of Two Security Software Packages

Function	RACF	ACF2
Data set protection	Protects by exceptions. Each data set is defined by a manual transaction or by using the "Automatic Data Set Protection" feature.	Protects by default. All data set accesses are monitored. User must take action to "unprotect" his or her data.
Protection implementation	Defines protection by individual data set and tape volume.	Defines protection by access rules applicable to all data.
Running in disabled mode	System must ABEND the user or bypass all security. Recovery involves manually reentering transactions.	Can continue data set protection via operator intervention, thus allowing orderly system shutdown without security bypass.
File access mode	Uses pseudo-VSAM requiring special systems utilities for backup and recovery.	Uses standard VSAM with standard IBM systems utilities to maintain the data base.
Reporting	Offers no reporting tools.	Provides several standard reports for monitoring access violations and data base changes.

Operational Acceptability. DP managers tend to view a security system as pure overhead because it does not directly contribute to the bottom line. Therefore, the software selected should impose as little overhead expense as possible on the target system and its users. Unfortunately, many security software packages consume such a large portion of system resources that they degrade system performance to an unacceptable level. It is critical, therefore, that the potential user carefully define operational criteria for system selection. Among the areas of concern in developing such criteria are:

- Resource consumption—The user should define the maximum acceptable levels for consumption of resources (e.g., hardware, software, personnel) for the software package. These levels should take into account any unusually high demands that may be made on system resources (e.g., demands of peak processing periods and critical response and rapid turnaround times).
- Operational degradation—Acceptable levels of operational degradation should be established, reflecting both user and system processing requirements.
- Ease of installation and implementation—The physical installation of the software package is separate from the implementation of the security controls offered by the package. The user should define the capabilities the proposed system must possess in order to permit quick and easy implementation of security controls by user personnel. In addition, vendor personnel should be able to install the package with a minimum of customizing.

- Expandability—The system should be expandable to cover additional data sets and files. In addition, changes in systems software (e.g., new operating system releases) should not make the security software system obsolete. The chosen security software should allow full upward compatibility and expandability.

Documentation and Vendor Support. The user should specify that the system and user documentation supplied by the vendor be both comprehensive and readily understandable by its intended audience. The vendor should provide a copy of the object code. The documentation should enable user personnel to readily implement and operate the system without extensive vendor intervention.

Because of the critical role of security software, the vendor should provide a high level of support. The potential user should carefully evaluate the vendor's past performance in support of the product. For new product offerings, the user should establish criteria for evaluating the support proposed by the vendor as well as the vendor's overall record of support for other products.

IDENTIFYING EXISTING DATA SECURITY SOFTWARE

In order to translate functional and technical criteria into a set of procurement alternatives, the potential user must understand the various types of data security software packages currently on the market. The user who has gained a basic understanding of security software can then begin the process of evaluation, selection, procurement, and implementation.

Secure Operating Systems

The basic concept in secure operating systems design is the security kernel. The security kernel mediates the access of all active system elements (people or programs), which are referred to as subjects, to all system elements containing information (e.g., files, records, data bases), which are referred to as objects. All of the security-related functions of a conventional operating system are collected into a small, primitive operating system called a security kernel. The three essential characteristics of this security kernel are:
- Completeness—All accesses of all objects by all subjects are checked by the security kernel.
- Isolation—The code that comprises the kernel is protected from modification or interference by any other software in the system.
- Correctness—The code performs the functions for which it is intended and no other functions.

Most of the development work in secure operating systems has been conducted by the Department of Defense in support of military and intelligence-related computing requirements. As a spin-off from this work, TYMSHARE, of Cupertino, California, has developed a secure operating system called GNOSIS for commercial applications.

GNOSIS. This capability-based operating system is designed to run on machines with an IBM System/370 architecture. The 370 architecture was chosen because it includes a wide range of available CPUs, extending from very small to very large configurations. A second consideration was that the 360/370 architecture has become an implicit industry standard and is expected to have a very long operational life.

In GNOSIS, every application, and, in fact, most of the operating system itself, is divided into small, self-contained units called domains. Domains communicate with other domains via explicitly authorized communication paths called capabilities. Domains are created and supervised by a very small kernel of system code. A GNOSIS domain serves the same purpose as does an address space or a virtual machine in other systems: it provides a place for the program and its data to exist and to execute. The difference is that a GNOSIS application typically consists of several domains, each containing a small subsystem (typically 50 to 1,000 lines of source code) that implements a special function.

Each domain holds capabilities that allow it to communicate with a small number of other domains. It is impossible for a domain to access its capabilities directly or to counterfeit the ability to interact with another domain. Thus, a domain may only interact with those domains for which it has been given a capability to interact. The same compartmentalization into domains has been applied to the operating system, so the difference between the operating system and the application is blurred; in fact, since almost everything except the kernel is in domains, there is no monolithic operating system. This arrangement makes it possible to replace application code selectively. If an application module is not performing properly, it may be safely replaced without jeopardizing the remainder of the program.

The GNOSIS kernel performs some of the tasks usually assigned to the supervisor. The kernel is very small (about 10,000 lines of code as opposed to 500,000 lines in some of the large IBM operating systems) because it implements and enforces, rather than defines, security policy.

The major significance of GNOSIS is that it is the first commercially available, fully supported kernelized operating system for a large-scale machine. Because of the high cost of replacing an entire operating system and the inevitable conversion problems, only those installations that require a level of data security considerably higher than normal commercial requirements should consider GNOSIS.

Access Control Software

The increased interest in software security and the growing realization that most existing operating systems are not very secure has led to the development of a number of security software packages designed to enhance the existing access control, transaction monitoring, and audit reporting features of current systems. These packages, unlike secure operating systems, do not fundamentally alter the software architecture of the target system. Although a number of these packages (e.g., RACF, ACF2, SECURE) are currently on the market and each performs in a somewhat different manner, they have certain basic functions in common.

Access Mediation. This function enforces controlled access to system resources and data, based on access rules defined by the user. Attempts to access any protected resources or data are intercepted, checked for legitimacy of access authorization, and then either terminated or accepted for execution.

System Auditing and Logging. Attempted violations of access rules are reported to the system managers, either through operator alerts (for serious breaches) or through logging and audit reporting procedures (for violations of lesser severity). Most of these systems audit a number of security-related functions, and this audit trail serves as a permanent record of these system transactions:

- Accesses—The system monitors who accesses what. Accesses and access attempts can be logged and reported.
- Violations—The system monitors who attempts what. Attempted violations can be logged and reported.
- Modifications—The system monitors who changes what. Modifications to data (e.g., add, change, delete, extend) are logged and reported.

File-Encryption Software Packages

Recent experience has amply demonstrated that existing software and hardware protection mechanisms (including access control software systems) are highly susceptible to subversion, particularly by insiders having detailed knowledge of the systems software. Therefore, increased attention is being given to using software packages for encrypting data. These systems operate on the principle that even if the access control mechanisms are breached and unauthorized users gain access to data, the data will be unintelligible. Two types of file encryption software systems are currently on the market.

Symmetric Cryptosystems. Most of these systems are based on the Data Encryption Standard (DES) established by the National Bureau of Standards (NBS). These systems are called symmetric because they use a single key for both encrypting (coding) and decrypting (decoding) data. This key is then stored in system tables, where it is protected by the operating system. Unfortunately, subversion of operating system controls can compromise the key.

The key can also be stored in encrypted form using the master key of the host system. When the data is decrypted, the data key is decrypted first by the host master key. Access to the master key gives access to the data key, however, and thus to the stored data. This approach requires that two parties who want to share a private communication must first both have the key. Key distribution is usually handled manually by courier or registered mail—a complicated process if keys are changed frequently. In addition, the key is exposed to compromise while in transit.

Asymmetric (Public Key) Cryptosystems. The most recent development in commercially available software cryptosystems is a new class of systems called asymmetrical or public key systems. In these systems, encryption and decryption are governed by different keys. It is impossible to derive one key from the other by mathematical computation.

Each user of the system is initially given a pair of keys. When one key is used to encrypt, the other must be used to decrypt, and vice versa. One key can be placed in a public directory available to all system users, while the other key is kept private. When two users communicate, the sender encrypts the communication, using the public key of the recipient, who then decrypts the message, using his or her private key. Even if an unauthorized user is able to breach the operating system's controls, the only thing found is the public key directory, which is common knowledge anyway. Without the recipient's private key, the unauthorized user cannot decrypt the communication. This approach provides a very high level of data security and is implemented in a small applications software module that is completely independent of the operating system.

EVALUATION AND RECOMMENDATION

Selecting a data security software package should be a thoughtful and orderly decision process. Although the size and nature of an organization may dictate how formalized this evaluation process will be, all organizations should perform the steps discussed in the following paragraphs.

Selecting the Evaluation Team

The personnel who will screen and evaluate the software packages should be carefully selected. No matter what the size of the organization, executive DP management should be actively involved. Among those who should be on the evaluation and selection team are the:
- DP Manager
- Programming Manager
- Operations Manager
- Data Security Manager/Security Officer
- Auditor
- General Counsel
- Contracting/Purchasing Manager

Soliciting and Evaluating Vendor Responses

The potential user should request that vendor responses to inquiries and solicitations take the form of written technical proposals or proposed statements of work. These documents can range from simple descriptions of the vendor's products, services, and support personnel to in-depth presentations of the vendor's corporate structure and overall management philosophy. These responses may include detailed tutorials to inform (or snow) the potential user regarding the extent of the vendor's knowledge in a particular technical area. Therefore, vendors should be encouraged to keep their responses short and to the point. Much bitter experience has shown that vendors who produce the most elaborate proposals are sometimes marketing oriented rather than engineering oriented—to the ultimate disadvantage of the user. The evaluation team should concentrate on several key portions of the vendor's response.

Statement of Capabilities. This should demonstrate the vendor's ability to deliver the needed software security system. Specifically of concern to the potential customer is evidence of:
- Adequate financial resources, as demonstrated in the vendor's audited financial statement
- Ability to comply with the required delivery or performance schedule, taking into account all existing business commitments
- Satisfactory record of performance
- Satisfactory record of integrity and professional ethics (particularly important when dealing with security)
- Necessary organization, experience, operational controls, and technical skills
- Necessary equipment and facilities
- Qualified personnel
- Identification and description of resources needed for proposed work, including vendor- and customer-furnished equipment and facilities

Technical Approach. This should demonstrate the vendor's understanding of the customer's requirements by:
- Formal technical definitions of requirements
- Identification of technical problems involved in meeting any requirements
- Alternatives or options, with a discussion of feasibility studies or risk analyses
- Technical descriptions of recommended solutions or alternatives

Management Approach. This part of the vendor's response should include an overall project management plan reflecting the organization of the project and related schedules. The formal steps required to complete each of the tasks described in the technical approach section should be specified, and plans for quality assurance and cost controls should be included.

Evaluation Findings. All proposals should be evaluated individually against the organization's functional and technical criteria. The results of the evaluations should then be compared to select the most acceptable proposals. The final evaluation of a proposal may be in narrative form or may use a numerical rating scale. A narrative rating should incorporate a summary of the proposal and a description of all advantages, disadvantages, and risks (both technical and other) associated with it. Using a numeric rating scheme, however, is a better approach. Generally, the technical and managerial portions of the proposal are considered to be most significant and are assigned weighting factors accordingly. In order to prevent bias in scoring, the evaluation team should not be informed of the weighting factors beforehand. Those proposals found to be technically acceptable should then be evaluated against the established cost criteria.

Test and Demonstration

Once the screening process has produced several candidate packages, arrangements should be made to demonstrate the capabilities of each through an operational test. A representative subset of the organization's data and/or processes should be used to test the adequacy of each system's controls. It is preferable to do this testing at the user's site, using the equipment and personnel that will be involved in the operation of the system. If this is impractical, however, and testing is to be performed at the vendor's site, special care must be exercised to ensure that test conditions duplicate the user's operational environment as closely as possible. The user should carefully plan and closely monitor the testing. The test plan should exercise the software according to the evaluation criteria. Samples of all reports (e.g., violations, transactions, audit trails) should be generated. Attempts to circumvent the system should be made as well as attempts to "hang" the system by purposely creating error conditions. These tests should be carefully documented. The system should be crashed to simulate recovery procedures used in case of system failure. A live test with actual system users should be conducted to evaluate user acceptance of the package. Resource consumption and response-time degradation should be carefully monitored and recorded for each system tested.

Final Selection and Recommendation

Based on the results of the evaluation and testing, the evaluation team should be in a position to select a package that meets the needs of the organization. The paramount factors in the final selection are:
- Ability of the software to satisfy specific functional and technical criteria
- Performance in operational testing
- User reaction and acceptance
- Overall capability of the vendor to supply and support the package
- Cost to implement, operate, and maintain
- Time, personnel, and system resources required for implementation

The evaluation team should then compile these findings and the team's recommendations into a final report and forward it to executive management for review and action.

CONCLUSION

Data security software can provide significant enhancement to the security of any computer system; however, a careful evaluation and selection process is needed to ensure that the package chosen will fulfill the organization's needs. First, the organization must have a set of well-defined system security requirements on which to base the selection. Then, functional and technical evaluation criteria must be established. An evaluation team should examine the available packages, solicit and evaluate vendor responses, and test the packages chosen. This evaluation process can help ensure that the software security package will provide full security benefits and will function properly in the organization's environment.

⑬ Good Data Center Housekeeping   by John W. Mentzer

INTRODUCTION

Users, management, and visitors often judge a data center by its appearance. The cleanliness and orderliness of the center and the employees' work habits can make a lasting impression. The DCOM should ensure that this impression is positive. In addition, the center's appearance can influence the effectiveness and efficiency of the data center.

A review of the data center's housekeeping procedures can help the DCOM to identify problem areas and work to improve them. In the highly automated environment of the data center, it is easy to overlook housekeeping details, many of which require manual efforts. These efforts, however, can increase the center's productivity, improve employee safety and morale, and give the data center a better image in the organization.

EVALUATING HOUSEKEEPING PROCEDURES

The checklist in Figure 13-1 can be used to evaluate the appearance of the data center. The DCOM should score each item based on his or her perceptions of how a visitor would evaluate the center. The checklist in Figure 13-2 can be used to rate the center on the quality of some procedures and safety measures that would not be seen by a casual visitor but can affect the productivity and safety of the center. Using this checklist, give the center four points for each Excellent, three points for each Good, two for each Fair, and one for each Poor. Divide the total of these scores by the number of items checked. A score higher than 3.0 is something to be proud of. The DCOM should review the items that were scored less than excellent to determine whether improvement is feasible.

MAKING IMPROVEMENTS

It is probably unnecessary to improve all items on the checklist. In addition, a center may need improvements in areas other than those listed. The purpose of the checklist is to stimulate thought about data center housekeeping.

Item	Excellent (never happens)	Good (sometimes happens)	Fair (usually occurs)	Poor (always occurs)
1. Surplus or broken furniture in data center				
2. Tapes, canisters, straps on top of drives				
3. Disk covers on top of drives				
4. Printouts or card decks scattered at random in the data center				
5. Dusty equipment or furniture				
6. Operator and maintenance manuals not stored in proper place				
7. Newspapers and magazines at the console				
8. Dirt or food stains on the floor				
9. Paper clips, rubber bands, tape rings on the floor				
10. Surplus disconnected equipment in the data center				
11. Extra floor panels in the data center				
12. Floor panels not in place (and no one working on installation)				
13. Broken equipment				
14. Personal appearance of operators				
a. Dress				
b. Sense of purpose				
c. Presentation of answers to questions				
d. Attitude toward visitors				
15. Trash in the area				
16. Fire drill information not posted and current				
17. Smoking in the data center				

Figure 13-1. Data Center Appearance Checklist

Item	Excellent (never happens)	Good (sometimes happens)	Fair (usually occurs)	Poor (always occurs)
18. Visitors not questioned upon entering the center alone				
19. Secure areas not secure				
20. Tape library disorganized				
21. Equipment or supplies in access ways				
22. Obsolete information on bulletin boards				
23. I/O areas cluttered				
24. No pattern to equipment layout				
25. Spare parts not stored properly in data center				
26. Equipment covers not on equipment				
27. Printers in use with covers up				

Figure 13-1. (cont)

An improvement campaign may occasionally require extensive outlays of time and money. For example, it may be necessary to rearrange the equipment to facilitate a logical, orderly work flow. Such large expenses may not fit into current data center plans; however, many improvements can be made with minimal costs through a sincere commitment to the project. How much can be done depends on the need for improvement and the resources available.

Action Plan

Housekeeping improvements can best be accomplished through a team effort. This is an opportunity for all personnel to be involved in a project in which the results are noticeable. The first-line supervisors and personnel in each functional area and each shift should also be involved. The role of project leader should be assigned to a person on the floor. The DCOM should develop a plan including lists of actions to be allocated to the different shifts and functions. Figure 13-3 is a sample action plan; names and estimated dates of completion should be added for each task on the list.

The initial action plan should not contain an overwhelming number of tasks. As the effort gains the support of the employees, however, other tasks should be added. The DCOM can use existing company policies and award systems to give recognition for positive actions. Awards for time- or money-

Item	Excellent (always occurs)	Good (usually occurs)	Fair (sometimes happens)	Poor (never happens)
1. Are floors cleaned on a regular basis?				
2. Are printer ribbons changed according to a schedule?				
3. Is tape drive cleaning part of the operators' routine?				
4. Is air conditioning maintenance scheduled?				
5. Does the center adhere to a regular computer maintenance schedule?				
6. Is an underfloor cleaning program performed annually?				
7. Is the halon system checked periodically?				
8. Are fire drills carried out in an orderly manner?				
9. Is there a maintenance schedule for noncomputer equipment (e.g., tape cleaners)?				

Figure 13-2. Data Center Maintenance and Safety Checklist

saving suggestions, mention in the organization newsletter or bulletin, and, most important, personal thanks and positive comments help to emphasize the importance of the cleanup effort. Some type of competition between shifts may also be helpful.

Shift Turnover Procedures

One of the major obstacles to a clean environment is the reluctance of people to clean up after someone else has left the area in poor condition. This is particularly true in a multishift environment. "This is the way I found it" becomes the common complaint, and soon everyone accepts the disorder as normal. One strategy for counteracting this tendency is to make housekeeping part of the shift turnover procedures. The DCOM can assign each shift some specific cleanup tasks and create a turnover check-off sheet listing the items that must be completed. Housekeeping items that should be performed daily or on a less frequent but scheduled basis should be added to the turnover log (see Figure 13-4). Once a clean area becomes the norm, it will be a matter of pride for employees to keep it that way.

Item	Responsibility	Estimated Completion (Days from Start of Project)
1. Announce cleanup and improvement project. a. Publish intent. b. Request suggestions and participants.	DCOM	1
2. Select team members on each shift. Select functional representatives.	DCOM	7
3. Develop initial action list.	Action teams	10
4. Select immediate "quick kill" items.	Action teams	11
a. Remove excess furniture and equipment.		14
b. Install all equipment skins.		17
c. Return all tapes to library at end of shift.		17
d. Order tape storage rack.		10
e. Install tape rack for storage of temporary tapes near drives.		33
f. Add housekeeping status to turnover log.		10
5. Review vendor maintenance procedures.	DCOM and administration	15
6. Generate vendor-related action list.	Action team and DCOM	20
7. Add valid suggested actions to list.	DCOM	Weekly
8. Publish status.	Action teams	Weekly

Figure 13-3. Housekeeping Improvement Plan

VENDOR COOPERATION

Equipment vendors may be partly responsible for sloppy conditions. For example, vendor representatives often neglect to put equipment kick plates in place on installed devices because the equipment will be moved again in the near future. Such shortcuts should be discouraged; the DCOM should only accept complete, timely equipment installation and maintenance from vendors. In most cases, the vendors will follow the standards set by the DCOM.

In addition to supplying contracted services, each vendor should pay proper attention to the physical appearances of the center. Floor panels not in place; spare parts, cables, or manuals left lying around; or disconnected equipment not removed promptly are inexcusable from a vendor. Such carelessness only occurs if the DCOM permits it. The DCOM should provide vendors with the center's rules for maintaining the environment and should clearly outline what is expected from the vendor to comply with these rules.

Cleaning Services

The center should have a schedule for cleaning services, whether they are provided by a vendor, a building cleaning service, or the company's own

Media
    Tapes stored properly?   _____
    Disks stored properly?   _____
    Disk covers in place?   _____
    Cards or trays stored properly?   _____
    Other _____   _____

Equipment
    Operator cleaning routines performed?   _____
    Maintenance completed as scheduled?   _____
    Equipment orderly and in proper location?   _____
    Other _____   _____

Miscellaneous
    Turnover logs complete?   _____
    Facility cleaning schedule complete?   _____
    Manuals and training aids returned to proper location?   _____

Comments

_____

_____

_____

_____

_____

_____   _____
Outgoing Supervisor   **Incoming Supervisor**

Figure 13-4. Shift Turnover Log—Housekeeping Procedures

maintenance department. The DCOM should discuss the cleaning process with the cleaning service and make the center's expectations clear. There should be a mutual understanding of how, what, and when cleaning will be accomplished. All environmental and safety systems, such as air conditioning, fire prevention systems (e.g., halon, sprinklers), and power systems, should have preventive maintenance and test schedules.

PERSONNEL PROBLEMS

Some housekeeping problems may stem from lax personnel management. To improve this aspect of the center, rules of acceptable behavior may need to be developed and observed. Paper clips, rubber bands, balled-up paper, and the like may simply be signs of carelessness; however, they may also be signals that data center personnel have idle time to play games. Unprofessional actions or attitudes should be discouraged, and the DCOM should develop methods to effectively utilize employees' spare time. The DCOM may wish to examine the center's staffing requirements and assign additional work to idle personnel or use spare time for in-house self-instructional training. Game playing by one or two individuals may also be part of a performance problem that should be addressed.

OTHER PROBLEMS

Another housekeeping problem that is often ignored is the habit of laying tapes, printouts, disk pack covers, lunch bags, clothing, and the like on flat equipment surfaces. This is unsightly and can affect the equipment's performance. Storing such items on top of the drives can interfere with the air flow needed for constant operation.

Other housekeeping requirements that may be included in this cleanup effort include the following:
- Operator cleaning procedures for printers and tape drives
- A systematic tape cleaning and replacement program
- A regular printer ribbon replacement schedule
- A standard stipulating that printer hoods must be kept closed to reduce noise and paper dust (This is particularly important if the printers share the same facility as disk, tape, or processing equipment.)

Storage Space

The improvements discussed in the preceding sections should incur minimal costs; however, the DCOM may find that inadequate storage space for a growing data center is one cause of poor appearance. If this is the case, the DCOM may need to buy cabinets for storing such materials as cleaning supplies, vacuum cleaners, or the operators' personal items. Adequate storage will be well worth the investment, since it will provide additional space in the equipment area and facilitate a smoother work flow.

Ongoing Effort

If the improvement effort is to be more than a simple cleanup to impress today's visitors, it must be an ongoing process strongly supported by the DCOM. Once the desired improvements have been achieved, the DCOM must ensure that the facility maintains these standards.

CONCLUSION

Improving data center housekeeping practices can have a significant effect on productivity, employee morale, and the data center's image within the organization. For the improvement effort to succeed, the DCOM must fully support the project and ensure that the data center staff realizes its importantance. Using the checklists and sample forms in this chapter, the DCOM should:
- Evaluate current data center practices
- Develop an improvement plan
- Alert all staff members of the improvement effort

- Assign clear responsibilities for the improvements
- Monitor progress carefully
- Ensure vendor cooperation
- Provide for feedback and follow-up on improvements

Once problem areas are reduced, an ongoing, persistent effort by all shifts is necessary to maintain high standards.

The improvement effort should not involve great expense; it is an economical way to increase the safety, effectiveness, and efficiency of a data center operation while making the data center—and the DCOM—look better.

14 Environmental Control

by Herb Liebovitz
and Thomas J. Boyle

INTRODUCTION

In many organizations, the DCOM wears more hats than does any other DP manager. In addition to dealing with users and effectively managing people, production procedures, and equipment, the DCOM must maintain a computer room environment within narrowly limited specifications to keep sensitive devices and media functioning properly and to avoid the loss of valuable data. The major issues involved in maintaining a data center environment are:

- Temperature
- Relative humidity
- Air quality
- Static electricity
- Water detection

This chapter discusses these factors and provides suggestions for ensuring proper environmental conditions.

ENVIRONMENTAL PROTECTION FOR COMPUTERS

Most computer professionals know that if temperature and relative humidity levels are not controlled, the computer will go down. Other environmental problems, however, are less widely recognized. For example, high particle counts in computer room air can bring a computer down faster than improper temperature and humidity.

AIRFLOW

The proper distribution of airflow in a computer room is necessary to achieve required temperature and relative humidity conditions. The typical computer room airflow is produced by dedicated air-conditioning units. Air circulates into the room through the raised floor by means of grills or perforated tiles and cable holes. It is then drawn up through filters into the ceiling ducts. If a central air-conditioning system also supplies air to the room, this air should be filtered and preconditioned to match the temperature and humidity of the air from the dedicated system.

The upward airflow removes heat from the room and inhibits lateral air currents, thus preventing the migration of contaminants from printers to other equipment. Good circulation also prevents the formation of hot spots in which the air surrounding a piece of equipment is warmer than recommended levels.

Air Velocity

Proper air velocity is also needed to maintain correct temperature and relative humidity levels. Inadequate velocities can lead to insufficient throw and poor circulation, while too high a velocity can disperse dust and create drafts. Air velocities should be kept between 20 and 30 feet per minute.

Fresh Air Supply

Unfortunately, fresh air often produces more problems than benefits. For example, unfiltered fresh air can admit dust and other contaminants in levels that are harmful to hardware. Unfiltered fresh air from an industrial area may carry particles that are extremely harmful to the hardware (e.g., crystalline materials). Ferromagnetic particles are attracted to magnetic media handling equipment, causing disruptive damage. Metallic and carbonaceous deposits on printed circuit boards can cause cross-tracking and short circuits. When the volume of fresh air exceeds the volume of air circulating in the computer complex, the variation in outside conditions can overwork the air-conditioning system and lead to improper temperature and relative humidity levels.

TEMPERATURE AND RELATIVE HUMIDITY

Room conditions should be maintained within equipment manufacturers' limits (usually 70°–72°F and 50%–55%) to ensure that temperature-sensitive components and humidity-sensitive materials (e.g., magnetic media, stationery) perform as designed. One major problem in maintaining proper levels is the failure to allow for future increases in DP equipment when designing the air-conditioning system. Additional DP equipment can quickly erode the ability of an air-conditioning system to produce the temperature and relative humidity levels it was designed to maintain.

Additional heat loads strain the system and cause hot and cold spots that could be improved somewhat by better balancing; however, the root of the problem is usually inadequate overall cooling power. Many problems associated with downtime can be directly attributed to CPU overheating; yet this is one item most frequently overlooked when searching for the cause of downtime.

Humidity

Improper humidity levels can cause static voltages on the floor and on nongrounded items—including personnel. Paper supplies and magnetic media function better when humidity levels are kept between 50 and 55 percent. In addition, proper humidity levels help prevent cross-tracking within the CPU. Some humidifiers can generate and release abrasive salts and fungal growth into the airstream. Crystalline salt particles can be particularly harmful to tapes and disks. To prevent these problems, it is necessary to maintain humidifiers in good repair.

AIR QUALITY

The advent of computers and other high-technology equipment in such areas as aerospace, bioscience, and medicine created a need for methods of ensuring clean conditions within a particular environment. The need for maintaining control of airborne particles in these environments led the United States government to develop federal standard 209B, which defines air cleanliness classes for various types of clean rooms.

The standard states that a computer room must be a class 100,000 room—it should not contain more than 100,000 particles, 0.5 microns in size, per cubic foot of air. The following requirements adapted from the standard should be enforced in all computer room environments:

- Clean room or clean workstation areas—These areas are to be operated with emphasis on minimizing airborne particle contamination to levels within the limitations indicated in air cleanliness classes.
- Environmental control—Such environmental conditions as temperature, humidity, pressure differential, and airborne particle count shall be controlled and recorded and these records regularly reviewed.
- Clean room air pressure—All clean rooms shall maintain a pressure above that of surrounding areas to ensure that all leakage shall be outward.
- Air change rate or airflow—Either the air change or the airflow velocity shall be specified.
- Temperature and humidity range—The temperature and humidity ranges shall be established as demanded by the products and in consideration of the personnel occupying the area.
- Microbial contamination—The allowable airborne microbial contamination shall be controlled to the level specified in an applicable process or product specifications. It must be recognized that airborne microorganisms are particulate in nature and are included in the total particulate count of air cleanliness classes.
- Other environmental factors—Due consideration should also be given to such environmental factors as light level, electromagnetic radiation, ionizing radiation, radioactive particles, and especially gases and vapors (e.g., mercury and cleaning solvent fumes). Adverse environmental conditions—for example, the presence of hazardous materials—are mentioned only to alert the user to the need for adequate controls and may involve conditions beyond the scope of standard 209B.

Environmental site audits have shown that rooms deviating from these general requirements usually have some type of computer malfunction. The level of ferromagnetic particles, carbonaceous particles, paper dust, and, in the case of laser-beam printers, toner dust has risen to the point where contamination has caused head crashes or CPU problems. Where the airborne particulate count becomes extremely high, microbial contamination is also common. This is indicated by a higher frequency of headaches and colds among computer room personnel than among their counterparts outside the computer room.

HEALTH PROBLEMS

An air-conditioning system should provide clean and comfortable environmental conditions; however, if it is not maintained properly, an air-conditioning system can create health hazards. The Swiss Medical Society has researched the effects of air conditioning on personnel. They found that absenteeism resulting from lung and bronchial infections is 20 percent higher among those working in air-conditioned areas. The researchers felt that continually recirculating air through humidifiers produces ideal conditions for harmful bacteria and fungi [1]. These health problems can be avoided by regularly cleaning humidification or condensate pans with a bactericide and fungicide to prevent the sludge buildup in which these organisms thrive. Contamination also comes from outside air introduced into the computer room through a duct system. Ducts are a perfect breeding ground for bacteria because they are dark, humid, and dirty. The DCOM can check this by looking at the air-conditioning diffuser in the computer room. Dark spots around the diffuser indicate an overload condition in the duct work could be causing problems. Keeping the inside of the ducts clean is almost impossible, and many ducts are never cleaned.

The duct work system should be cleaned at least once a year as another preventive measure. In addition, environmental probes should be placed in the ducts to continuously measure the level of contamination. An environmental site audit of one data center revealed such high levels of three types of bacteria in the condensate pan and duct work that the computer room was deemed unsafe. This is an extreme case; however, when data center absenteeism increases, the DCOM should check the bacteria level.

HARDWARE CONTAMINATION

Hardware contamination is an endemic problem in data centers. Some blame for this problem can be traced to the manufacturer who carelessly applies paint on hardware surfaces. Paint particles can be found in most equipment. In addition, if the particulate levels in the computer room are too high, the inside of the equipment will probably be contaminated with ferromagnetic particles that collect on magnetic media, carbonaceous particles that can cause cross-tracking, paper dust that can harm hardware and people, and iron oxide (rust) that rises from the floor plenum. Any particle greater than 30 microns in diameter can cause disruptive damage to hardware. The DCOM can open the back of the CPU to check for accumulations of dirt or dust. If deposits are evident, a person should be called in to determine the extent of the pollution and the type of particles.

WATER DETECTION

Many computer rooms have water leakage problems. Some have experienced floods. Any leak adversely affects temperature and relative humidity levels and may cause water damage; however, too few computer rooms are protected against such problems. Often, the building design places water pipes above the computer room ceiling or bathrooms on the floor above the computer room. In addition, maintenance of dedicated room air conditioners is often so poor that condensate pans overflow.

Overhead water leaks are easy to spot, but a subfloor leak can cause damage for some time before becoming apparent. Computer rooms with water detection systems usually use point sensors. These detectors are excellent if the leakage occurs where they are located. Since most point sensor detectors operate on batteries, the protection is lost if the batteries are not replaced when necessary. A water detection system that provides area protection is more effective. A zoned perimeter strip detector system uses a tape attached to the floor over a wide area. The tape contains conductive water-sensitive wires that activate an alarm when water is detected. This type of system offers wider protection and does not depend on batteries.

MICROWAVE TRANSMISSION AND MAGNETIC FIELDS

Microwave transmission or magnetic fields near hardware and data carriers can disturb or even erase recorded information. Organizations sometimes neglect to check for magnetic fields and microwave transmission when selecting new computer room sites. Consequently, tape and disk drives do not function properly.

If the disturbances result from outside microwave transmission, an aluminum shield may have to be built around the computer room.

Magnetic fields can originate from equipment within the computer room. For example, the voice coils on disk drives throw off magnetic fields in excess of the recommended levels. In fact, the label on one manufacturer's disk drives warns the user not to bring tapes or disks within six inches of the voice coil box.

Magnetic fields can degauss tapes and disks and result in loss of information. A gauss meter examination should be conducted to prevent this. If the magnetic fields are strong enough to harm tapes and disks, work areas or equipment should be arranged so that the fields do not interfere with the normal work flow pattern of tape and disk use.

STATIC

Static usually results when the humidity in the room drops below the manufacturer's recommended criteria. The extremely dry air allows excessive electrostatic voltages—generally caused by friction—to accumulate. In addition to being extremely uncomfortable for personnel, these voltages can cause hardware problems (e.g., select locks on disks) and mutilate information held in core memory.

The easiest way to minimize this condition is to maintain proper temperature and relative humidity controls. Another preventive measure is completely grounding the computer room floor by developing a floor-grounding grid. The static dissipates over the grid, preventing unnecessary damage to the equipment.

CONCLUSION

To avoid hardware contamination and failures, damage to stored data, and health problems caused by improper environmental conditions, the DCOM should be aware of all the factors discussed in this chapter and ensure that they are controlled. This entails scheduling regular maintenance and cleaning of the air-conditioning system, balancing the placement of equipment for maximum air-conditioning efficiency, and monitoring the levels of essential environmental conditions. By following the suggestions discussed, the DCOM should be able to ensure safe environmental conditions for both computer equipment and data center personnel.

References

1. "Air Conditioning Fever." *Heating and Air Conditioning Journal*, Vol. 49 (September 1979), 12–15.